COMEDY

*The Mastery of
Discourse*

This book is dedicated to
James Drewery, who taught
me the real power of the
unconscious mind.

COMEDY

The Mastery of Discourse

Susan Purdie

HARVESTER
WHEATSHEAF

New York   London   Toronto   Sydney   Tokyo   Singapore

First published 1993 by
Harvester Wheatsheaf
Campus 400, Marylands Avenue
Hemel Hempstead
Hertfordshire, HP2 7EZ
A division of
Simon & Schuster International Group

Typeset in 10/12 pt Palatino by
Columns Ltd, Reading

Printed and bound in Great Britain by
Biddles Ltd, Guildford and King's Lynn

British Library Cataloguing in Publication Data

A catalogue record for this book is available from
the British Library

ISBN 0–7450–0723–6 (hbk)
ISBN 0–7450–0724–4 (pbk)

---

1 2 3 4 5 96 95 94 93 92

Contents

Acknowledgements

The intelligence, knowledge and generosity of my friend and colleague Jeff Collins have contributed to every stage and every page of this book.

Many friends, colleagues and students have contributed insights, criticism and support; I am especially mindful of Kate McGowan's living proof that politics, theory and joy in life go together. Colleagues in my department supported an initial sabbatical term that launched the project, my institutional library, especially Barbara Parry, assisted beyond the call of duty, and my son Cory Peters was amongst those who supplied me with joking material that lady lecturers might not otherwise encounter. Jacqueline Jones, my editor, helped greatly with the organisation of a complex argument.

PART ONE

Joking as Discourse

Introduction

This book investigates what is happening when someone finds something funny. Since that occurs in response to extremely diverse material, in differing circumstances and to degrees that vary from uncontrollable guffaws to the merest apprehension of wit, many distinctions can be made within and around this experience. I am seeking a unifying thread that can be recognised as present, to some extent, whenever any element of funniness is identifiable in our response to anything. I shall use the term 'joking' to designate all these occasions – including social exchanges, textual comedy, and any other event which elicits the kind of response I shall always refer to, for convenience, as 'laughter'. I term the characteristic effect created through joking and registered in laughter 'funniness', to avoid the simply celebratory connotations of 'humour'; for my argument investigates the problems inherent in joking's inseparable, simultaneous generation of both pleasure and power.

Joking occasions are not only diverse but widely valued and very common. This suggests that they are an interesting and important topic, but it complicates their discussion in several ways. Joking is valued most obviously because laughter feels pleasurable and is associated with release from external and international restraints. I shall suggest that this increase is only half the story – that funniness involves at once breaking rules and 'marking' that break, so that correct behaviour is implicitly instated; yet in transgressing *and* recognising the rules, jokers take power over rather than merely submitting to them. Since I shall argue that a fundamental 'rule' – whose marked transgression actually constitutes joking as such – is that of language, and since I shall draw a line through the theories of Saussure, Lévi-Strauss and Lacan to identify operating the basic 'Law' of language (Lacan's 'Symbolic Order') with experiencing full human agency (i.e. subjectivity), more appears to be at stake in enjoying joking than merely permitted high spirits. It is not surprising, therefore, that not only the capacity to receive and to produce joking but also the capacity to interpret it are typically laid claim to, promptly and fiercely, whenever the topic is proposed. The frequency and variety of its instances exacerbates this difficulty, since everyone can produce particular examples that apparently refute any generalisation about laughter. The eagerness with which readers are likely to counter every point in my argument can be taken as evidence precisely of the power I am identifying as the 'meaning' which joking fundamentally constructs, in all its occasions and prior to other effects. However, I must beg for a certain amount of patience, for the argument cannot be fully defended until each of its premises has been examined.

Both my provisional generalisations and any examples I offer are also, always, open to dispute because joking is so evidently overdetermined: in every good laugh there are literally innumerable elements, involving relationships within and between the material, personalities and circumstances involved. Indeed, since at one level joking invites a breach of the rules which usually constrain meaning, it is especially susceptible to the phenomenon whereby the more any utterance is scrutinised, the more meanings associated with it are found. Furthermore, joking is also overdetermined in the sense that most of its elements can *accurately* be described in several different ways. Much of what I have to say is therefore congruent with other analyses: it would be surprising if it were not. Since several good summaries of other theories exist,[1] I have not supplied another here, but for those readers already familiar with them I have tried to indicate major points of indebtedness or disagreement.

On the whole my argument should not be taken as trying to replace other theories but as augmenting and often unifying them in respect of one important factor. This is my claim that

joking paradigmatically involves a discursive exchange whose
distinctive operation involves the *marked* transgression of the
Symbolic Law and whose effect is thereby to constitute jokers
as 'masters' of discourse: as those able to break and to keep
the basic rule of language, and consequently in controlling
possession of full human subjectivity. It is on the back of this
effect that the social potency of joking rides. Joking not only
effects immediate discursive control but also appropriates
wider power because, implicitly, each particular usage a joke
negotiates is constructed as that which is rationally Law-
abiding. Hence the additional social power established by
denying other people's behaviour such propriety when they˙
form the Butt of joking.

Conversely, starting from the Butt, my model of joking can
be defined as the dynamic constitution of two discursive
relationships. Jokers form an excluding relationship with their
object. Amongst its many elements, joking sometimes involves
other persons as Butts who are *de-graded* from a perceived
position of power, but it always objectifies the Law which is
degraded in being successfully defied, but also reinstated
when its transgression is marked as such. This reinstatement
crucially defines the extent to which an utterance feels 'funny'
as opposed to utterances whose unmarked transgressions are
enjoyed in a predominantly poetic or phantasising mood. The
second discursive relationship is that formed collusively
between the joke's Teller and its Audience (of one or more),
which depends upon and creates their object's exclusion. This
generates a delicious intimacy, which is pleasurable and
powerful in itself, for important parts of the joking utterance
remain tacit – in some (e.g. 'punch-line' jokes) the actual
transgression is elicited but not articulated in the triggering
utterance; and in all joking the 'proper' usage, implicitly
established via mutually taking the joke's material to be a
transgressive *mis-use*, remains only silently affirmed – so that
the joking moment allows an unusual and potent joint
subjectivity. The triggering utterance that is produced by the
Teller and received by the Audience is only part of the total
utterance which constitutes a joke; that totality is produced in
the moment of the exchange, *between* Teller and Audience.

The major distinction between my own and most other

theories will now be evident: I take all joking to involve a
discursive exchange and (which is inter-implied) to negotiate
the use of language – allowing 'language' to designate all
formulable signifying structures, not only verbal systems.[2] On
the contrary, Freud, for example, follows a common distinction
in separating verbal and conceptual 'wit' from 'the comic',
declaring the former but not the latter to require a Teller and
implicitly assuming the distinction of funny events – someone
doing something laughable – from funny words. That distinction is also implicit in the two major traditions of 'superiority'
and 'incongruity' theories;[3] the former concentrate upon the
power of laughing at an inferior person, the latter upon the
manipulation of words or concepts into unlikely but suddenly
acceptable juxtapositions. These theories concentrate upon the
discovery of funniness and, like Freud's, focus on its
invention; they direct attention to the nature of any trigger
such that it is likely to be laughable; one consequence is that
the implicit paradigm which emerges focuses on one individual
finding something funny. In relation to this, the linguistic
structuring implied in *making sense* of any events – which is
self-evidently involved in finding them funny – is overlooked.
Because I have started from the question 'What happens when
someone finds something funny?', my focus is upon the
reception of joking rather than its inception and, as I said
above, I have been led from this to a model in which
discursive exchange forms the paradigm of joking and solo
laughter appears as a derived and unusual instance, a version
of 'talking to yourself'. In taking the exchange of joking
intention as the activity which actually constitutes funniness, I
see the Teller's function as more than that of handily
supplying material one might not find oneself, and the
Audience as doing significantly more than only (as Freud
suggests) confirming an already constituted joke. Freud's work
was a central starting point for this book (the other was
Stallybrass and White's *Politics and Poetics of Transgression*,
which is discussed in Chapter 7), but my project – to explore
the levels of the social process of joking – is different from
his.[4]

My emphasis on the discursive exchange centrally involved
in all joking contradicts not only the model of most theorists

but that of most 'people in the street'; and that *mis-taking*, itself evidence of joking's subjective potency, is examined in my first chapter. In the rest of the opening chapter I shall examine the fundamental 'rule of language' whose breach is the first condition for the reception of any utterance to feel 'funny', and then the relationship of that rule's observance to subjective agency. Utilising arguments which present operation in the Symbolic as, thus, deeply potent yet always psychically precarious suggests why joking's uniquely *marked* breaches of its Law have such powerful effects. In the second chapter I shall demonstrate that such a transgression can be identified in every joking exchange, although other factors are usually involved and often more conspicuous. My third chapter then considers the relationship which emerges between the Symbolic Law and personal or institutional targets, as forming 'the object of joking'.

Part Two – Chapters 4, 5 and 6 – carry this analysis to literary and especially dramatic 'comedy'. I am not claiming that all comedy texts are only funny, or that they consist merely of funny events interpolated into 'straight' stories, but that recognising in comedies the joking presentation of a particular *behavioural* 'language' – the discourse of exchange – is crucial to useful treatments of the genre. I argue that comedy presents its action as a species of discursive exchange, and that this is achieved by the affective distancing that has often been recognised as characteristic of the genre. Following this argument, it appears that the persistent structures of comedy may be most clearly described in terms of patterns of characters representing the possibilities of ab-using this language of exchange.

Finally, in Part Three, I shall consider the sociopolitical implications of identifying all joking as discursive exchange and therefore finding an appropriation of discursive power to be an element which is essential to it, not the mere contingent effect of selecting *disadvantaged* targets. In particular, issues of gender politics, already present in my title in the term 'mastery', appear here, because our patriarchal culture identifies discursive power with masculinity. At the same time, I take a generalising view of the pattern which conflates whatever is called 'masculine' with valuations of legitimate and competent authority while the opposing label 'feminine' constructs a lack of institutional and/or essential power. Without ignoring the particularity of different experiences, this construction of what is feminine as a negation of, rather than an opposition to, what is masculine must, I believe, be recognised as one of the fundamental semiotic operations by which patriarchy similarly maintains the advantage of 'white' over other ethnicities, of heterosexuality over homosexuality and of capitalism's winners over its losers. The experience of all those occupying the lower circles of this pattern is similar in that it involves socio-economic disadvantage as well as a difficulty in forming a subjectivity independent of the structure which defines personal value as something awarded by definitionally different individuals. I use the term 'abjected' to suggest this common positioning in patriarchy of what is not 'properly masculine'; and I argue that in joking the formal confirmation of accepted discursive proprieties will tend to reinforce existing structures of exaltation and abjection, independently of particular contents. The social potency which is consequently constructed in all comedies, whatever their story treats, is, I shall suggest, masked by most literary-critical theories. My final chapter considers treatments of the genre which, in taking its defining characteristic to be a concern with 'vital forces' (not discursive norms), construct the texts as *benevolent* arguments for accepting 'life as it is'.

A study of joking, then, can be seen to highlight the problematic relationship between a necessary and desirable individual empowerment and the destructive exercise of power over others, in a culture where 'power' is primarily understood as identical with aggression.

Notes

1. McGhee (1979, pp. 4–39) contains a wide-ranging catalogue, including approaches within the social sciences, by Patricia Keith-Spiegel; Howarth (1978, pp. 1–21) offers an intelligent summary of philosophical and literary treatments of 'laughter' and 'comedy'. Heilman (1978, pp. 254–63) offers 'A Brief Survey of . . . various twentieth-century works . . . earlier sources often referred to . . .

the contents of several anthologies in the field'. The most inclusive anthology of approaches, Lauter (1964), is out of print at the time of writing this book. Corrigan (1981) and D. J. Palmer (1984) comprise selections of literary theorisations and include summarising introductions; in Chapter 8 my reservations about assumptions made in these volumes are explored.

2. This definition is expanded in Chapter 2 in the definition of the rule of 'same and different' whose observance constitutes, in this sense, language-use.

3. Plato, Sidney, Hobbes and Bergson are prominent examples of superiority theorists; Beattie, Kant, Schopenhauer, R. W. Emerson, Arthur Koestler and Jonathan Miller all offer incongruity approaches.

   Hobbes's succinct formulation may summarise the first theory's emphasis on the fact that laughter elevates the laughers above other people: '*Sudden Glory*, is the passion which maketh those *Grimaces* called LAUGHTER; and is caused either by some sudden act of their own, that pleaseth them; or by the apprehension of some deformed thing in another, by comparison whereof they suddenly applaud themselves' (p. 125). Freud's approach to 'the comic' (see Note 4 below) is a form of superiority theory.

   Schopenhauer, by contrast, exemplifies the alternative emphasis upon the solitary cognitive process of laughter: 'the source of the ludicrous is always the . . . unexpected subsumption of an object under a conception which in some respects is different from it' (quoted in Lauter, p. 359).

4. Freud focuses on the Audience in Chapter 5 of *Jokes and their Relation to the Unconscious*, 'Jokes as Social Process', where he notes that the fact that it is an Audience, not a Teller, who actually laughs at a joke presents problems to the theory he has thus far elaborated – of psychic economy (in the play of words or of concepts) permitting normally inhibited behaviour. His conclusion is that

> telling my joke to another person would seem to serve several purposes: first, to give me objective certainty that the joke-work has been successful; secondly, to complete my own pleasure by a reaction from the other person upon myself; and thirdly – where it is a question of repeating a joke that one has not produced oneself – to make up for the loss of pleasure owing to the joke's lack of novelty. (1905/ 1960, p. 156)

The essentially discursive nature of joking is virtually implicit in this chapter, and it has already been suggested earlier, in the notorious discussion of 'smut' (pp. 97–102), which has been discussed by Mehlman, Neale and Weber as Freud's approach to a theorisation of discourse. Those who know it will recognise that I am much indebted to Freud's book. However, Freud does not in fact restate his central focus upon the initiating individual. He goes on, in Chapter 6, to elaborate that commensuration of 'Jokes, Dreams and the Unconscious' which is surely his primary intention in writing the book, and finally turns in his last chapter to the wholly non-discursive account of 'the comic'.

Freud's book is one of several influential theorisations of laughter which have been produced either as incidental items amongst a catalogue of human affects (like Hobbes's succinct definition) or as a 'stalking horse' towards some other and implicitly more important understanding. The latter group, besides Freud, includes Bergson's *Le Rire*, which actually expounds a totalising philosophy of 'vitalism', and Koestler's discussion as an introduction to his theorisation of *The Act of Creation*. These tangential approaches suggest the curiously taboo nature of funniness, at once highly valued and marginalised, as well as a potential unwillingness to confront its nature directly and thus uncover the 'policing' action which precisely depends upon camouflaging its operation.

Amongst Freud's major works, this is also the oddest. As his translator and editor Strachey notes (pp. 5–6), it is the only major work which received virtually no revision; while at several points arguments appear to be redirected in ways that might elicit revision. A small but telling example appears on page 94, where Freud announces that he 'will select the most innocent possible example of a verbal joke', tells it, and then continues: 'since, however, doubts arise in me after all as to whether I have a right to describe this joke as being non-tendentious, I will replace it by another one'; which he does. At the same time – as Strachey, Gilman and others have pointed out – Freud had been collecting jokes, but specifically Jewish jokes, for many years. Gilman offers a detailed and plausible reading of the work as Freud's unconscious attempt to distance himself from his disadvantaged ethnic origin by respeaking it in the dominant discourse of science. Certainly its unpolished state, along with the fact that Freud worked on it at the same time as he was writing the *Three Essays on Sexuality*, leaves it open to reinterpretation whilst also leaving its implications incompletely pursued.

In 1927 Freud wrote a short paper on 'Humour' which suggests another aspect of my own model: the operation of joking to confirm a sense of self. However, he specifically restricts that formulation to 'humour', distinguished from other kinds of joking. Apart from this, Freud always referred to jokes within the triptych of manifestations of unconscious activity: 'Jokes, Dreams and Parapraxes'. As with Lacan's similar treatment, this emphasis on the unconscious origins of jokes is distinct from my own interest in their discursive effects.

1

Joking and Discourse

Joking as Discursive Exchange

I am using the term 'joking' to designate all 'occasions of funniness' because it seems to be the best possible within available vocabularies. Unfortunately, it entails possibilities of confusion with one particular set of instances involving the sort of utterances that are commonly labelled as 'jokes' because they are intrinsically constructed to be funny. I shall return later to the internal mechanisms which promote this effect, but it is useful to remember that any utterance can be 'a joke' in my own, wider sense, even if the circumstances in which that could happen are fairly improbable. We can 'get' private and purely circumstantial jokes because (self-evidently) we understand that they *are* joking; and when they are delivered they are usually accompanied by external signals of this, such as changed voice tone. Formulaic jokes are effective not simply because of their intrinsic mechanisms but because they carry internal signals (including those mechanisms) that they are uttered within 'a joking intention', and they too are usually delivered with additional, external signals of this. Noticing the necessity of identifying a joking intention within the process that produces funniness leads to recognising the essential discursive exchange at the heart of joking. From that vantage point we can consider what occurs when someone does, really, laugh alone; and why that comparatively rare event should be assumed as a frequent and even paradigmatic instance.

It is in fact possible to recognise a joking intention in

something someone says (or does), and yet not be moved to laughter. That can happen in various circumstances which can all be variously described, but basically this utterance will not have elicited thinking that in itself transgresses the fundamental rule of language. We may well note that the *utterance* is itself socially transgressive – for example that it contains or implies an obscenity – but we will not feel funniness unless we reproduce the transgression, in our own minds, as momentarily 'permitted'. So when recognised joking fails, the external or internal inhibitions usually remain unambiguously in force; and while some sort of rule-breaking is 'marked', it has not genuinely been committed by the Audience. A rarer instance of failed joking occurs when an utterance is clearly signalled as a joke, yet contains nothing that we experience as transgressive: sometimes we just do not get the joke, probably because we lack some information (such as a particular obscene term) on which its mechanism depends. Sometimes we are presented, especially if we are parents of small children, with utterances clearly using signals of joking intention that have in our perception no transgressive implication at all – such as 'Knock, knock – Who's there? – Tomato – Tomato who? – Tomato sauce'. Yet other small children (and perhaps drunks) will find those utterances funny, not only because bringing to mind that viscous substance tomato sauce feels transgressive to them, but because in the right circumstances the most basic assumption that the rule of language is being breached, implicit in an understood joking attention, can itself have the effect of transgression. (Additional circumstances and effects may be involved in any of these examples: even at its simplest, joking is always overdetermined.)

When, however, we genuinely entertain a transgressive thought in our own minds in response to an utterance that we understand as joking, that understanding leads us to mark the transgression as such at (virtually) the same moment. When that happens, it feels funny and we (usually) laugh. Our appreciative response does, of course, (as Freud noted) assure the Teller that their joke works and that the often implicit transgression has been transmitted; but this response, and the transgression which it signifies, is itself received back by the Teller in a way that constitutes a further communication. In accepting the 'laugh' as a proper response to the trigger, the Teller confirms the transgressive thought as, nevertheless, constituting part of a meaningful discursive exchange, so that it is held within the bounds of the Law. That is possible because the originally understood intention to joke has produced the 'mistake' as marked; thus the proper rule which the error is agreed to breach is itself stated tacitly between Teller and Audience. When something is funny, it has not only allowed us thinking usually prohibited, it has also offered an immediate confirmation that our thinking is meaningful: that is, our thinking is of the kind that creates the 'agency' of producing utterances which are received as effective. Hence the necessity of the Teller lies not in their producing potentially laughable material but in their reception of our signalled transgression, which confirms that this actually constitutes an observance, and not only a breach, of the Symbolic Law.

It is certainly possible to take something someone says as unintentionally funny. Here, of course, the speaker is the Butt of joking, constructed as genuinely incompetent, while the laugher 're-presents' the utterance to themselves, at once incited to reproduce the perceived error and affirming their own capacity, in marking that, to produce 'proper' utterance. Solo laughing involves constructing oneself as Teller and as Audience in a way that is similar to the construction of oneself as both Teller and Butt when one 'laughs at oneself'. It is even possible to laugh at yourself, alone, and so construct all three discursive joking positions autonomously. Laughing at your-self is fairly obviously a derived and unusual instance of something that paradigmatically occurs between separate individuals; and so, I am arguing, is laughing 'with' yourself. Any solo laughing, however, involves considerable confidence in one's own propriety on the particular site where it occurs. Those who frequently, genuinely, produce it are likely to be people whose general identity is formed across competence in language-use – the academics and intellectuals most likely (in any era) to produce theorisations of joking.

For most people, genuine solo laughter occurs more rarely

than they think. Often we note an utterance as a potential trigger and store it to repeat to others; and even when real and spontaneous laughter is elicited inadvertently, we are very likely to seek external confirmation as well. Yet most people share the theorists' assumptions that it is the normal, basic form of joking. When an example of what is laughable is invited, it is most frequently an event (someone *doing* something) that will be stipulated, and since such joking apparently involves no language, it seems evidently to involve no Teller. However, those exemplary events are very probably instances of comic performance: if they are not recollections of specific performance, they are usually mishaps – like the epitomal man who slips on a banana skin – that are not frequently encountered outside performance and not likely to feel funny when they are.

I shall defer (until Chapter 3) the issue of laughter arising more easily when we know that a victim is not truly hurt, because it does not involve an absolute distinction between performed and real events. That distinction lies in performed events actually having a Teller. At the simplest level, performers themselves 'utter' the pratfalls or gaffes which make us laugh. These are not genuinely mechanical movements or exhibitions of lack of self-knowledge, but skilful representations of them. When we are in the theatre we know that the inept stage character is a construction, competently communicated to us. If we do genuinely laugh at a real event, we are surely re-presenting it to ourselves in the same way as we retell inadvertently funny speeches, as jokes, to ourselves. In noticing that performed events are utterances we see that they involve (again at the simplest level) an operation of a signifying structure, within which the performers' actions 'make sense' as events which may be funny. In direct parallel, real events can make sense only within linguistic constructions. An event is funny when it makes us think transgressively as well as – in the schema outlined above – marking our transgressive thought. This is much more likely to occur in the context of a performance, and when real events genuinely cause laughter we have effectually 'textualised' them in attending to their conceptualisation before their real effect in the world.[1]

When we laugh at performed events, we really know that a Teller is both inciting and receiving our transgressive response: comic performers (and authors) are seeking the laughter which is unknown or unwelcome to their characters; but at the same time, in most performance, it is easy and pleasurable to suppress awareness of the presentation and attend directly to its re-presentation of events. Therefore it is easy to remember or imagine what is performed for us as if it were real, and theorists from Plato and Aristotle to Bergson and Freud seem to do that in their discussions of 'unselfknowing', 'grotesque', 'mechanical' or 'excessively effortful' individuals who are, thereby, comic.

This book lays stress upon the linguistic manipulation involved in all joking, and its dynamic affirmation of jokers' capacity to use language 'properly' – through the double action of genuine but marked linguistic transgression – because it is in that operation that I identify the fundamental and ambiguous potency of joking: in this light, joking appears as central in the construction of Symbolic agency. Even at an anecdotal level the way solo laughter is taken as a frequent occurrence, together with the common suppression of the discursive exchange that joking, like all language-use, must paradigmatically involve, demonstrates how eagerly any con-struction of Symbolic power is pictured as autonomous. Laughing alone, I argue, is an experience derived from interpersonal exchange which actually occurs quite rarely, but is remembered as comparatively frequent precisely because such instances represent a maximum of discursive power-taking. This chapter will go on to investigate why this 'power of self' can be experienced only through others' recognition of it, and some of the reasons why we tend to deny this.

That the control and exercise of language equates with power is almost so obvious an observation that it may escape investigation. Yet it is possible to reunderstand the power of language-in-use, if identifying discursive capacity with the experience of full subjectivity leads us to understand why such a desirable state is so difficult to maintain. Recognising the linguistic basis of subjectivity exhibits it as precarious, but always striving to find itself assured.

The 'Rule' of Language

The theories of Saussure, Lévi-Strauss and Lacan on which this chapter draws have been rehearsed many times in English academic publications, yet they remain not merely contentious but considerably misunderstood on this side of the Channel. Part of my project is to demonstrate, to those readers who are not familiar with them, that they are coherent and useful. I also want to make prominent a particular 'through-line', in which the rule-base that Saussure establishes as the most fundamental condition of language relates directly to Lacan's conception of the Symbolic domain, where he locates full human agency. I should emphasise that this is therefore an interpretation rather than an account of this work, which omits much – especially the consequences for therapeutic psychoanalysis that are always Lacan's own primary focus – and introduces my own formulations, especially the formulation of the rule of 'same and different'.

Lacan equates our subjectivity with our operation of language, within a particular process that gives rise to both as identical effects of the constitution of the unconscious.[2] By locating this process as a response to irreconcilable psychic demands, his theories suggest at the same time why this empowering competence nevertheless remains unstable and tensely held. Since this formulation uniquely illuminates the attraction of experiences (including funniness) which in one way or another relieve this tension, it seems well worth pursuing, despite the difficulties of finding clear understandings of Lacan's writings and the problems – notably of gender evaluation – that appear during the search.[3]

The concept of subjectivity which Lacan claims to be constructed in using language differs from that of identity, in that the latter implies a set of characteristics (e.g. predispositions, memories, intentions) attached to and distinguishing an individual. Subjectivity implies the condition of self-awareness such that one feels oneself to *be* 'a person who can have a human identity. If everything that 'makes sense' involves mental representation within language, then it is not very contentious to claim that we know our identity within language. Lacan's claim that subjectivity arises wholly as a *function* of using language is more fundamental. It produces a specific formulation of that primary potency which is conferred by a mastery of Symbolic language, prior both to the social control such mastery commands and to those allocations of cultural prestige which can be instated by control of linguistic designations. In the most basic sense of the term, 'proper' people are those who can produce 'proper' language and, in a reciprocal negotiation, whatever is produced by 'proper' people is taken to define 'proper' language at every level, from the rationality of belief to the orthodoxy of grammar.

When he presents subjectivity thus as the effect of a competence which young humans acquire through interaction with other people, Lacan is opposing that deep strain in Humanist thought which assumes the 'self' to be an autonomous, given essence; but in this respect he is not unique.[4] His originality lies first in the equation of subjectivity and language-use and, beyond this, in identifying the child's movement into language-use with the specific psychological stage postulated by Freud as 'the Oedipus'. If I understand his project correctly, Lacan is thereby offering a material explanation of the nature of language as a product of the child's necessary relationship with those who nurture it.[5] To understand his theories, it is necessary to grasp the theory of language that he is using.

It is in the work of Ferdinand de Saussure that the linguistic theory underlying Lacan's work first appears. Its most widely known stipulation defines language as the use of 'signs', which consist of two elements: the signifiER – usually defined as some mark, sound, or other material event – and the signifiED – designated concept; which are joined or 'clipped' together, like the two sides of a piece of paper, to form a sign. That this connection is 'arbitrarily' formed by social convention is not a particularly radical assertion.[6] However, Saussure's further stipulation – that signifiers and signifieds are both constituted only as 'values' within the linguistic structure – is potentially much more disruptive of commonsense assumptions.

Saussure declared: 'the conceptual side of value is made up solely of relations and differences with respect to the other terms of language, and the same can be said of its material side' (p. 116). This makes 'signifieds' something quite different from any material reference that they may entail. Even when we name something directly, we are signifying a construction of concepts and never merely pointing at the object. Naming what is now trying to jump on to my lap 'a cat' involves making sense of her as a locus for a complex of ideas many of which (e.g. 'pet', 'pest', etc.) are not intrinsically founded in her material being; and all these conceptual constructions, here intersecting to form one signified, can be recognised as significant values only as they are the same as and different from others in what finally becomes an endless, interconfirming structure that is one's understanding of experience (cats are living, not inanimate; animals, not plants; domesticated, not wild; companions [pets], not food, etc.). Thus Saussure observes:

> even outside language all values are apparently governed by the same paradoxical principle. They are always composed:
> 1. of a *dissimilar* thing that can be *exchanged* for the thing of which the value is to be determined; and
> 2. of *similar* things that can be *compared* with the thing of which the value is determined. (p. 114)

Given this, the implication of identifying signifieds as well as signifiers as 'values' is that thinking is linguistically structured (a fuller statement of the point I made above: that 'making sense' always involves linguistic constructions).[7]

The operation whereby we identify these significant values was most fully elucidated by Roman Jakobson, who as a linguist was primarily interested in the formal qualities of language, and worked predominantly upon verbal systems. It was, however, through Jakobson's detailed and objective demonstration that 'discriminations of binary difference' account for the whole complex operation of constructing sounds as meaningful speech that Claude Lévi-Strauss conceived his 'structural anthropology', which identifies cultural behaviour as a parallel linguistic pattern of meaning construction. Lévi-Strauss's seminal influence on Lacan, in turn, led the psychoanalyst to develop the implications of Saussure's stipulations in relation to the individual human mind in ways which may be more clearly apparent when they are approached through these earlier formulations.

Jakobson developed a systematic description of the process whereby the meaningful units of speech (the phonemes: roughly sounds – that make up lexemes: more roughly, words – out of which spoken utterances are built) are recognised as such through their discrimination from other sounds within that set of sounds which can be meaningful in a given 'tongue'.

This may be described as the operation of the rule of 'same and different' – a meaningful sound is one perceived as significantly the same as certain others in belonging to the system, but also as significantly different from them in specific ways.[8] Jakobson's work offered a precise formulation of how Saussure's 'values' come to operate in relation to the phonemes of a specific tongue. Rather ironically, Jakobson's work on verbal phonetics suggested to Lévi-Strauss the possibility of extending the concept of 'language' beyond verbal structures and beyond the formalised 'sign systems' Saussure had indicated as relevant to the concept. He applied Jakobson's theory of language to cultural behaviour that had been investigated since the nineteenth century by anthropologists – such as kinship structures and 'totemism' – as well as to those hitherto regarded as too trivial for scientific notice, such as dietary categorisations. Lévi-Strauss's radical move was to interpret these precisely as 'languages', first of all in exhibiting the structures that Jakobson had elaborated in phonetics. In cultural phenomena Lévi-Strauss identified systems where elements are discriminated through their intersection of specific binary qualities (e.g. natural/cultural, untransformed/ transformed), just as Jakobson had shown phonemes to be recognised as specific combinations of vocal scales (loud/soft, open/closed).[9]

I think that implicit in Jakobson's work, and crucial to Lacan's use of it, is the assumption that 'language' does not depend upon the existence of a set of signifiERs which are of an intrinsically different nature from their signifiEDs. That is a specific quality of certain structures, notably of verbal language, which are consequently capable of very complex meaning. In the most fundamental structures, however, the basic 'elements' (i.e. whatever is discriminated) can come, in certain occurrences, to 're-present' each other. A sign is constituted – meaning is generated – whenever any two elements are recognised as 'same and different', such that one semantic space is occupied by one specific element that is immediately present and another specific element that the first 'brings to mind'.

A fundamental rule of language can be proposed in relation to this: that meaning depends upon restricting elements to appearing singly in each semantic space – only one element taken as a signifiER clipped to only one element recognised as its signifiED.

Making sense occurs as the condition of delimiting elements that are also held in relationship to one another. Just as speech cannot make sense unless any recognised phoneme is held to exclude every other at that point, so no signing can happen 'properly' if one signifier generates more than one (*incompatible* – definitionally different) signified. Such multiple generation of signifieds is, of course, precisely what initially happens in many aberrant uses of language, including poetry and joking: for this is the rule (as I shall elaborate in Chapter 2) which joking definitionally transgresses; but unless this excess generation is then recuperated in some way, all 'meaning' threatens to disappear, because the crucial separation of what is signifying from what is being signified will finally collapse.

Only in particular cases is it possible to see language as a system which 'carries' some distinct thing – meaning – separated from its vehicle, like the load inside a lorry; and such cases are misleading because they assume that meaning can be unloaded from language and exist somewhere separate from it. If we see that all signifiers and signifieds are 'values', we see that they are all, always, identifiable concepts which become associated with material embodiments. Lévi-Strauss developed Saussure's perception that language consists not in 'naming' things but in constructing concepts within chains of 'same and different' *which are 're-presentable'*.[10] Lacan developed a recognition that language occurs as the operation of holding one element as separate from another with which it is also

associated (and not, fundamentally, vice versa). I am suggesting that this fundamental separation is put in question
whenever any distinction of elements is threatened; that all
aberrant uses of language play with such separation, but that
joking, by marking its transgression, creates mastery of the
basic 'one for one' rule. The material phenomena involved in
the systems Lévi-Strauss describes render the productive
model of language somewhat more approachable than it is in
Lacan's parallel model, where mental constructs that have no
determined material embodiment come to function as signifiERs – and thereby produce, and so *determine*, the possibility
of all signifiEDs, including the self as a subject (as 'The agency
of the letter in the unconscious or reason since Freud' [in
Lacan, 1977a], for example, insists).

To take a simple but not wholly trivial example: all cultures
classify foods and particular combinations of them in relation
to classified events; it is not merely excessive provision but
specific kinds of food which 'belong', for example, to specific
feasts and in an obvious way carry connotations of those
feasts: in England, but not in France, turkey is associated with
Christmas; while for the French, but not for the English,
smoked salmon carries that connotation. More fundamentally,
if we start from a binary distinction between 'nature' and
'culture', we can notice that food is for humans the transformation of what is natural into what is cultural, and Lévi-Strauss
elaborately charts relationships between the cooking methods
which effect that transformation and the cultural categories
with which they are associated: his particular focus is upon
those mediating methods which are ambiguous in being
partly a human transformation of the foodstuff but also partly
a co-opted, wholly natural process – such as rotting, smoking
or collecting honey. He finds these associated with specially
discriminated cultural categories – with what is 'holy' or
'taboo'. His assertion is that ambivalent foodstuffs have
representational relationships with cultural categories that are
ambivalent in, similarly, being constructed as partaking of
both human culture and forces outside it. Elements in the
different chains thus represent each other because they are
'like' in transgressing definitional boundaries, and – a
fundamental point – these mediating elements are specially

discriminated because within them the distinctions within the binary categories are actually constituted. Thus the initial priority of signified categories over categorisations that represent them is reversed: the classification of food is what produces, rather than being founded upon, the distinction between 'nature' and 'culture'.

The meaning of such structures can be described as an exhibition of the mathematical relationship of ratio, which is a double relationship where the relationship of one (set of) elements to another is in turn related to that between another set: as the relationship between the numbers four and six is related 'in ratio' with that between the numbers two and three. Operations of ratio allow chains to represent each other, as in football colours; if red and blue are distinguished as values in the chain of colour, and Arsenal and Chelsea are similarly distinguished as values in the chain of clubs, red can represent Arsenal and blue Chelsea. Honey marks the distinction between natural and culturally transformed stuff, as ritualised behaviour in general marks that between natural (animal) and culturally transformed (human) behaviour in general. In this way elements become 'representational' components that can be described as 'language', in structures far prior to the institutionalised understandings in which football clubs can be formed with elected insignia through which supporters advertise their allegiances.

The meaning with whose production Lévi-Strauss is primarily concerned is not any kind of message but the act/possibility of 'meaning' itself. The term is attended to as an intransitive verb, so that what is important is not that 'I mean X' when I utter language, but that 'I am meaning'. What is primarily constructed in language-use is the human mind, as a subject who is, in every inter-involved sense of this term, 'meaning-ful'.

This understanding emerges in Lévi-Strauss's first distinctive work, *The Elementary Structures of Kinship* (1949), in which he 'solved' the long-standing anthropological conundrum of kinship structures and their associated prohibition of incest.[11] He describes this system as 'the exchange of women' and then identifies women as functioning within it 'like signs', whose effect as exchanged 'values' is to constitute the exchanging groups as such. Lévi-Strauss's own – arguably confused – formulation is considerably clarified by interpreting it in the way Lacan did; thus the act of exchanging – structured through 'same and different' binary discriminations of gender, generation and marriage/blood kinship – can be seen as producing not the identities of the groups but (to parallel the distinction I have already made) their self-awareness as groups which can have identities. I shall return to this theorisation of exchange in my account, in Chapter 5, of the 'language' which comedy texts specifically negotiate. Lévi-Strauss goes so far as to suggest that this 'exchange of women' constitutes the very foundations of human culture as such, hence of language itself. This is specifically the formulation which influenced Lacan's 'Rome Discourse', which forms the crucial point in his work; here he proposes the identification of language-use with individual subjectivity, and also offers an ontogenetic account of the origination of language.

The paper delivered to the Rome Congress of 1953, enitled in full 'The function and field of speech and language in psychoanalysis', heralded Lacan's split from the international Freudian community and marks the vital extension of his earlier work on 'the mirror stage'. The 'mirror' now becomes the instigation of only one of three 'Orders' whose persistent interaction constitutes the model of the human mind that Lacan thereafter posits: the Imaginary, the Symbolic and the Real. Although many implications coexist within this model, some interpretations of it are definitely misleading. Despite its terminology of 'the Ego', recalling Freud's centrally self-conscious mental area, the mirror does not in itself constitute 'the subject', for that involves the construction of the signifier–signified relationship which appears later, as the Symbolic Order; equally, these are not designations of 'stages', for although the Symbolic appears later than the Imaginary, it does not replace this but is structured totally as an interaction with it: 'One will observe that the topology of the subject finds its statute only by being related to the geometry of the Ego' (1977a, p. 326).[12] Nor is Lacan's 'Real' much like Freud's 'reality principle', whose recognition constitutes maturity; it is that which is totally and intrinsically outside language, at once the 'suchness' of material phenomena and the absolute state towards which the mind strives. Increasingly metaphysically, Lacan comes to equate the Real with both death and the 'jouissance' of desire's total (impossible) fulfilment.

These three Orders, then, are all present in the post-Oedipal mind but, again, they cannot be seen as 'layers' or as separated areas which then interact, since their action is wholly in relation to each other, like a 'Borromean knot' composed of three rings, each of which binds the other two.

Although the account of the earlier 'mirror stage' which appears in *Ecrits* dates from 1949, Lacan first formulated it in 1936 and may originally have intended a reformulation of Freud's 'ego' as psychically central. His dispute, then, centred upon Freudian psychoanalysts' therapeutically supporting their patients' 'defence' of the ego, for Lacan here defines this as essentially and irreparably split. This is because it arises (he claims) from the infant's 'mis-recognition' of itself in its – literal – mirror-image. The image appears to be competent and coherent, while the infant's body is still uncoordinated and, until this moment, present to itself only as dispersed sensations. Hence the infant's 'jubilation' in forming 'an identification in the full sense that analysis gives to that term' (p. 2). This is to call on Freud's theory especially in relation to his formulation of a primary 'narcissism' (tellingly so named from the Greek myth of the young man who fell in love with his own reflection) which involves the investment into another object of the mind's own libidinal energy (primary force, understood by Freud as exclusively sexual).

Freud's point was that others are always desired 'like' or 'as' myself; Lacan's is that the 'I' (i.e. 'ego') is an 'imago' – a necessarily formed illusion – which is always desired as an 'other'.[13] The mirror's 'I' is thus an unattainable 'object of desire', constituted in 'the dialectic of identification' but still prior to the point at which 'language restores to it its function as a subject' (p. 2).

The Imaginary ego can experience itself only as plenitudinous or lacking, as present or absent (and its plenitude is illusory). Because language involves signifiers which 're-present' the signified, it constructs a negotiation of absence and presence; with access to the Symbolic's representational operation we can, with all sorts of effects, 'bring to mind' something that we recognise as absent. Lacan often refers to the *'fort–da'* game Freud observed in his grandson: the small boy repeatedly threw away and retrieved a cotton reel on a string, saying, with each movement, first 'gone' [*fort*] then 'here' [*da*] and so, as Freud noted, representing to himself his mother's absence and prospective return. Whilst the representational function of Symbolic language has all kinds of uses in conceptualising and thereby allowing (eventually) material control of our material surroundings, its primary potency in this context arises from its allowing an individual to represent itself to itself: 'I am me'.

This potency, and also its inherently troubled operation, arise from the Symbolic's constitution within a network of relationships that have been generated in the Imaginary following the 'mirror' moment: 'the inexhaustible quadrature of the ego's verifications' (p. 4). To extrapolate, the infant comes to recognise the M-other [*sic*] as another person whose attention bestows upon it the plenitude it has identified in the mirror-self, and so its desire is extended into the 'desire of the other': it desires not simply the mother herself, but to be what is desired by the mother. The value of 'the desire of the other' is that it is (the construction of) plenitude, a 'value' that can be produced only through relationship, as the values in two-dimensional geometry depend upon multiple relationships to other values. Fullness of self can similarly be constructed only through the attention of another on to whom fullness has been projected.

Lacan identifies this 'desire of the other' with what he terms 'the phallus', and I shall defer discussion of the difficulties this obviously creates until Chapter 7 in order to pursue the story of the infant which Lacan narrates in terms of Freud's Oedipus. At this point another figure, not the literal father but a figure of absolute power – the Name of the Father – is taken to be apprehended as forbidding the child to be the Desire of the M-other, on pain of annihilation (even Freud's account, which insists upon the specifically penile location of such a 'fear of castration', notes that parents' literally threatening this 'is not, after all, of universal occurrence; [we] will be driven to assume that children construct this danger for themselves, out of the slightest hints, which will never be wanting' [Freud, 1909; PFL, p. 172]). The child cannot, then, hold on to this desire (for Lacan, to 'be' the phallus, rather than sexually taking the mother); nor can it be relinquished, since it is invested with the child's own primary energy. The resolution is the repression of the phallus; so constituting an area of the mind which is fully active but genuinely and totally unavailable to consciousness. This is Lacan's description of the formation of the unconscious, which is also the genesis of language-use. That identity occurs because the phallus, in its repression, is constituted as 'a signifier . . . intended to designate as a whole the effects of the signified, in that the signifier conditions them by its presence as a signifier' (p. 285).

This puzzling and little-understood stipulation is the basis of all Lacan's subsequent work, and the reason for adducing his theory within a formulation of discursive power. It is clarified by taking note of the implicit and explicit references to Jakobson and Lévi-Strauss that are central in the 'Rome Discourse'. We have seen that in Jakobson's formulation, language depends upon the operations of binary discrimination which are multiply operative in constituting meaning; while Lévi-Strauss finds such multiply operating codes in cultural behaviour, generating a signification which is fundamentally the very possibility of meaning. The fact that the phallus is repressed as a signifier means not that it becomes a different kind of entity from the other positions present in the child's mind, but that its being repressed creates the relationship of 'same and different' between it and the other mental figures of self and desire. The two-dimensional geometry of the Imaginary's absence and presence is expanded into a three-dimensional 'topology',[14] where positions relate in doubled binary relationships, so that elements are distinguished from others in one chain and also related to others in another chain, as their 're-presentations'. The energy vested in 'the desire of the other' can be extended into different objects – they are 'the same', while at the same time they are 'different' – a relationship of signification, not identity, is made possible.

The repressed phallus functions as a *'point de capiton'* (literally, 'upholstery button': the button that anchors upholstery) – fixed point that locates the other contents of the mind, inasmuch as they all, ineluctably, involve desire, as representations of it: 'the phallus as signifier gives the ratio of desire' (p. 288). The primary meaning of subjectivity, 'I am me', is enabled. But since individual subjectivity is inaugurated by repression, it is always an enforced operation, threatened with breakdown from the ever-present energies of the repressed material which remains dynamically active, seeking to 'return'. The repression involves a loss of primary pleasure, of the Imaginary bliss of fully achieved plenitude; but it is crucial to retain this repression, since failure to do so is equated with annihilation.

We can see fairly easily that there is now an introjected rule or Law which is obeyed under the threat of 'castration'; and all the prohibitions which deeply condition behaviour (which have been described as 'natural law') can be equated with the primary 'Rule' of language: that what is 'same' and what is 'different' must not be confused. ('It is in the *Name of the Father* that we must recognise the support of the symbolic function which, from the dawn of history, has identified his person with the figure of the law' (p. 67)). When the projection of the self which is the phallus is repressed, the Name of the Father – in Lacan's phrase – 'bars' 'the desire of the other' from what is allowed to be self-awareness. Lacan connects this 'bar' with the line Saussure used to represent the relationship between signifier and signified, on the model of an arithmetical fraction; but where Saussure's emphasis is upon the connection between the two, Lacan's is upon their separation: the separation that is instated between the plenitudinous power and the other representations which remain in consciousness but are 'conditioned by it' as the 'whole effects of the signified'. The relationship of 'signifier to signified' is extended through the whole network of mental entities, because every element – starting with the Imaginary Ego and including the phallus – has been constituted only as the object of another's attention.

A signifier is 'meaningfully' produced not only because it relates to other positions and represents a signified, but additionally because it is exchanged with another *person* – whom we have constructed as 'significant' – hence Lacan's model of the mind as a topography, with multiple positions that can be moved amongst multiple dimensions, yet remain connected in the same spatial disposition.

This brings us to a characteristic of language that is self-evident in our most ordinary experience of it: the confirmation that 'I am meaning (anything at all)' lies in another person's reception of that meaning. At every level of experience, from the most mundane to the most obscure, 'my significance' – my being as a subject – is constituted by or 'in' others. Thus Lacan says that 'there is no speech [i.e. as such] without a reply' (p. 40); which his French editor glosses as the 'Formula of human communication: Human language constitutes a communication in which the emitter receives from the receiver his own message in an inverted form' (p. 329). This is founded upon the Symbolic Order's expansion, into representable multidimensionality, of the primary pattern of desire: 'man's desire finds its meaning in the desire of the other, not so much because the other holds the key to the object desired, as because the first object of desire is to be recognised by the other' (p. 58).

For Lacan the fundamental meaning 'received back in reception' is not whatever 'message' a communication may entail, but the confirmation of individual subjectivity; this parallels that confirmation of group-being which Lévi-Strauss identified as the primary product of the 'language' of the 'exchange of women'.

> For the primary function of language is not to inform but to evoke.
>
> What I seek in speech is the response of the other. What constitutes me as a subject is my question. In order to be recognised by the other, I utter what *was* only in view of *what will be*. In order to find him, I call him by a name he must assume or refuse in order to reply to me. (p. 86; emphasis added)

Thus we are 'subjected' under a 'Law' which operates simultaneously as a powerful threat forbidding what we are constantly tempted to do, but also as an 'order' which, when obeyed, enables us to speak with effect. This may be compared to the law in a court, which lets us speak when we obey it and silences us into 'non-persons' when we are in contempt of it. Lacan compares this psychic law with the 'Debt' Lévi-Strauss posits as the foundation of the 'exchange of women' – since that must begin with a 'giving away' separated from expected, later, 'returns'; and with Jakobson's notion of the 'primary . . . zero-phoneme' (p. 68). What begins as a 'lack' of psychic plenitude is transformed in the Symbolic, whilst it is always 'purloined' towards its Imaginary origin, into the structurally separating point of absence which produces the psychic and social potency of language.

It is now possible to see why the consciously discursive operations of joking are illuminated in relation to the operation of the Symbolic Law, though Lacan himself follows Freud in concentrating upon the irruption of the Imaginary that joking and comedy entail.[15] Because joking marks such transgressions on the site of their genuine occurrence, it confirms us strongly as able to keep the rule of 'same and different', as well as to break it. The effect of joking is emphatically to instate the law, and ourselves as those who master discourse in defining as well as producing the usages which conform to it. This is achieved through a collusive communication which is a paradigm of 'received reception', for through the tacit exchange involved in 'understood joking intention' a specific confirmation 'that I am Lawfully meaning' is created – the affirmation of Symbolic subjection established in the moment of its mutually marked transgression.[16]

Notes

1. The direct attention to language which all joking involves, and the consequent definition of 'a joke' (i.e. an object of laughter) as 'something that has no proper effect in the world', will be expanded in Chapter 3.
2. The most succinct summary of his post-1953 position is made in Lacan's slyly refusing Preface to Lemaire's putative account of his work.
3. Part of the difficulty of reading Lacan lies in his constant and often unindexed references; above all, his writings are saturated with references to the works of Sigmund Freud. Even apart from

this, what he is saying at any point almost always comprises a multiplicity of implications whose centre is constantly shifting.

Above all, the difficulty arises from the nature of language, which is in itself what he intends to convey. His work describes and is founded upon the perception that the nature of language is dynamically to produce entities which are apprehended as if they are prior to – and the producers of – the activity of 'meaning' which produces them as its definitional effect.

4. This strain may be traced back through the Judaeo-Christian formulation of the 'individual soul', and seen as opposed in the tradition of continental philosophy which issued in the Existentialism that crucially influenced Lacan.

5. Thus his claim is that the structure of language is experientially acquired: a much more far-reaching assertion than that supplied by the common-sense reflection that children have to learn its particular contents (words and other signs) from other people.

6. Medieval philosophers such as Aquinas accepted that words are not essentially connected to their meanings.

7. Since language's 'meaning' is seen to depend wholly upon the same–different relationships of elements within the signifying structures, and not to emanate from the relationship between some elements inside language and some others outside it (for it is impossible to 'know' these outside their linguistic construction), meaning is not a quality *discovered* in the world but one *constructed* in the mind. It is, I think, because this assertion is often 'mis-taken' that it is resisted. It is not a nihilistic claim that 'there is (really) no meaning', nor a version of the Cartesian scepticism, developed by Russell, that we are debarred from an ideal, 'true' knowledge of the world – quite the contrary. Nor is it a version of the solipsistic claim that 'nothing exists outside the mind'. Rather, it is the claim that *meaning comes into the material world through language-use*: language *is* what makes sense.

This does have implications for the nature of the human mind that manifests itself in language construction and the inherent instability of the 'self'; but these do not involve the auto-destructive 'death of the subject' in quite the way that is sometimes suggested. Psychoanalysis's postulation of the self as inherently 'lacking', Lacan's punning 'basket with a hole in the bottom', should not be confused with some literary critics' 'death of the *author*'.

8. Jakobson postulated a basic double discrimination in the energy – loud/soft – and frequency – high/low of sounds, operating in parallel across the primary distinction of open vowel sounds from

closed consonantal ones. Perhaps most fundamentally, he demonstrated that each sound's unique recognition operates through the
'minimal discrimination' which establishes its boundaries at the
point where, when its combination of qualities is altered in any
dimension, it becomes recognisably a distinct sound in that
system: compare the discrimination between 'l' and 'r', which are
physiologically and aurally continuous, in English.

9. The 'triangulation' of double oppositions which Lévi-Strauss
   adopted from Jakobson may be too simple to account for all
   phonetic or cultural discriminations. What surely holds good is
   the understanding that extremely complex semantic sites are
   'recognisable' through basic binary discriminations articulated
   across multiple dimensions.

10. This is masked because we often read representations of objects
    transparently, as if they were those objects; but of course we
    know that a picture of a chair, for example, is by no means
    identical with that chair. 'Part for whole' and 'whole for part'
    signifiers, even in the rare instances where the referenced thing
    itself is involved, are also not identical with what they signify –
    not least because of the distinction between 'referent' and
    'signified' developed below.

11. This theory is much more fully elaborated in *Structural Anthro-
    pology*, published in French in 1958, whence my account is
    drawn. (Lacan refers [1977a, p. 110] to the original French
    presentation of that essay in 1951). I mention the earlier date of its
    first presentation to establish the link between this work and
    Lacan's 1953 'Rome Discourse'. The relationship between the two
    men was, of course, a personal one.

12. All my quotations are taken from the 1977 English edition of
    Ecrits – pp. 1–7: 'The mirror stage as formative of the I';
    pp. 30–113: the 'Rome Discourse'; pp. 281–91: 'The signification of
    the phallus'; and p. 326: the 'classified index of major concepts',
    compiled by Jacques-Alain Miller and approved by Lacan.

13. Lacan's references to other species whose reproductive behaviour
    patterns are triggered by the sight of one potential mate suggest
    that he is also trying to fulfil Freud's goal of definitively linking
    human psychic formations with biological phenomena.

14. Topology is the branch of mathematics which deals with the
    articulations of surfaces in three (and multiple) dimensions.

15. Besides some specific references, in this context, in *Ecrits*, Lacan
    implicitly refers to the last chapter of *Jokes and their Relation to the
    Unconscious* (on 'Comedy') in his introduction to the *Four
    Fundamental Concepts of Psycho-Analysis*, and he returns to the

topic of comedy in the seventh 'Seminar' – again considering its
revelation of the unconscious, as Greek comedy, literally,
exhibited 'the phallus'.

16. A further link which motivated Lacan's application of Lévi-
Strauss's theory of kinship to psychoanalysis lies directly in its
treatment of the incest prohibition, which is also the site of the
Oedipus that (in *The Interpretation of Dreams*) formed Freud's first
specific elaboration of unconscious process: 'Isn't it striking that
Lévi-Strauss, in suggesting the implication of the structures of
language with that part of the social laws that regulate marriage
ties and kinship, is already conquering the very terrain in which
Freud situates the unconscious?' (Lacan, 1977a, p. 73).

2

Joking as the 'Ab-use' of Language

In Chapter 1 I traced through the work of Saussure, Lévi-Strauss and Lacan a fundamental rule whose observance, I argued, constitutes language-as-such: that at any given moment only one signifying element functions to represent only one signified element. In this chapter I want to demonstrate that all joking – in the wide sense I have given the term – involves a violation of that rule. Because signifieds are complex concepts they usually involve a lot of components, but these all accumulate to form the single signifier, as 'cat' entails a precise conjunction of animal, domestic, and so on; the most obvious violation of Symbolic Law consists in generating more than one *incompatible* signifieds linked to one signifier, but an 'excess' of signifier can also be seen as involving the same transgressive energies.

Joking violates all sorts of discursive proprieties, and its 'permission' of obscenity, aggression, and so on, is often far more conspicuous than its breach of the rule of language-as-such; but the connection I have traced between this Symbolic operation and subjectivity suggests why it is the *marked* transgression of this rule that potently, always, involves joking in exercising and reconciling contradictions inherent in our fundamental experience as 'meaningful' beings. Saussure's identification of linguistic 'values' being formed only as comparative points within each structure ('*x*' as 'NOT all the elements which are NOT-*x*') suggests that such excessive signification – sliding into a proliferation of meanings which destroys effective signification – is an ever-present possibility in language-use; and all our use of language thus reveals itself as tensely held, since the system intrinsically, of its very nature, constantly threatens to 'unravel'. Hence it is the primary 'buttoning' of the repressed Signifier (what Lacan calls 'the phallus') that enables any linguistic performance; yet because that is a *repression* of fundamental drives, its intrinsic nature is constantly to 'return' and find its satisfaction. Joking confirms our ability to hold on to Symbolic operation in the same moment as it allows a 'play' of the energies which militate against that.

Since the gain of fundamental psychic potency at stake in affirming our 'proper' operation of the Symbolic Law – prior to and underlying the social power involved in mastering specific discursive formations – is achieved with difficulty and at psychic cost, it is not surprising that a great deal of language-use violates that Law and produces pleasures which joking shares. Joking can be distinguished from the other aberrant modes with which it is closely connected to the extent that they 'permit' the Law's violation in different ways.

In phantasying mode, in night-dreams and day-dreams, the restrictions of designating structures and social codings are wholly suspended, and the distinction of one element from another – the opposition of absence from presence and of forbidding from permission – are dissolved, so that satisfactions denied within the Symbolic Order can be achieved. Joking and phantasy are directly connected, for its 'permission' of phantasy's transgressive thought is one of the most generally accepted pleasures of joking (I shall discuss this further below). It is, of course, central to Freud's treatment of jokes that the forepleasure of wordplay serves to lower inhibitions, constituting an 'innocent' pleasure which promotes the 'tendentious' objectives he defines as expressions of 'hostility, obscenity and cynicism'.[1] It is implicit in my own treatment of language that its manipulation is neither psychically nor socially 'innocent'; but further, joking as such can be distinguished from private or public exercises of prohibited language because the violation is marked and the resulting affect is funniness. In private phantasy as in 'purely' transgressive social interactions, the Symbolic Law is simply suspended: these are operations of the Imaginary and do not involve the Symbolic Order.

Similarly, in poetic mode, 'artistic' language may be valued precisely because it invites a proliferation of significations, and utterances that are treated as 'art' (in all media) also exhibit the 'other side of the coin' which appears in joking: an unusual attention to signifiers. This is transgressively excessive in terms of normal usage, since it threatens the operation of language in foregrounding the constructed and (in the technical sense of the term) arbitrary nature of all elements; so, paying attention directly to language, we skirt awareness that significant coherence occurs *only* in/as language. The pleasure of release from the rule that signifiers must attach 'in ratio' to signifieds – the obverse of the stipulation that signifieds must extend one at a time across commensurate signifying spaces – entails, again, the danger of destabilising the entity which is our own identity and surrendering subjective agency. However, what is poetic but *not* funny constitutes a discourse where excess language is agreed to be (anomalously) a proper signification through its recuperation to some sort of special 'truth' assumed to lie beyond 'ordinary' language; and so Symbolic operation is reinstated because the violation is taken as not really a violation.

To show that joking, as distinct from either poetic or phantasising discourses, always includes some marked transgression of the Symbolic Law – so that it fully breaches *and* fully reinstates that rule – is not to explain all jokes or any particular joke; that, for the reasons set out in the Introduction, is literally impossible. Good jokes are heavily overdetermined, containing many elements that can each and in all their interactions be described in differing ways; each telling of a joking utterance, even in a book, also involves a unique combination of personalities, relationships and circumstances. The funniest jokes provoke their particular Audience, at that moment, into a maximum of actual transgression, which is a matter of the particular circumstances and the skill of delivery, as well as the structure and content of the utterance. Often, the Symbolic violation defining joking utterance as such is a small part of what makes it *strongly* laughable to some Audience: taking Freud's model, the amount of hostility or obscenity we find ourselves enjoying in the initially elicited transgressive thought can be seen as our main pleasure. In concentrating on the *marked* breach of Symbolic Law as, nevertheless, the factor constituting joking-as-such, I am looking towards the particular discursive effects – inextricably psychic and social – mobilised in all joking, which are distinct from the aggression, etc., which may or may not express themselves through joking. I shall also consider how the social codes and symbolic hierarchies that are cultural expressions of what we individually operate as internalised inhibitions appear in joking in their aspect as linguistic structures: so that in joking their transgression is experienced as itself a violation of Symbolic Law.

I have already pointed out that any utterance can, in some circumstances, operate jokingly, but some utterances involve an intrinsic mechanism which constitutes them as especially constructed for the job. The work a joking mechanism performs is to 'trap' the Audience into a situation where their proper activity of 'making sense' inevitably entails producing Symbolic error. This is most obvious in verbal jokes, where a 'set-up' leads to a punch line that is in effect a puzzle. Whether it is the climax of a little narrative or the answer to a question, only actually producing a transgression will interpret the punch line in such a way that the utterance does make sense. Socially exchanged jokes – those utterances that are specially invented and repeated to create funniness – usually produce their mechanism within recognisable formulae which change like fashions in clothing: 'Have you heard the one about . . . ' is now, for example, distinctly passé, while various kinds of fake question have been popular for a long time ('How many x does it take to change a light bulb?' being superseded by 'What do you call a Lada when it's . . . ?', and so on). These formulae function, in conjunction with altered voice tone and other characteristics of physical delivery, to establish an initial joking intention. Within this, the more an Audience's attention is diverted from the fact that some violation of Symbolic Law is about to be elicited, the more genuinely that breach will be produced in their minds, and the funnier the total exchange will feel. Hence a deadpan delivery generally enhances joking, a pretence that the utterance is seriously intended; and an effective formulaic joke will be long and interesting enough to distract the Audience's expectation from the forthcoming 'error' whilst that, when it comes, will be sufficiently justified as a necessary completion of the utterance to hold its cognitive 'rightness' in balance with its Symbolic 'wrongness'.

The transgression will involve an excess of signification within a semantic space – that, marked as mistaken, is the minimal condition for recognisable joking; and the most obvious improper linguistic excess is probably the simple doubling of a verbal signified: a pun. In propitious circumstances, the following example has a good chance of being funny:

> Errol Flynn invited a group of friends to dinner and gave them . . . [here insert a long enough list of delights to suggest opulence and divert the Audience's attention from their approaching, 'understood' transgression – without losing their attention] . . . at last a dwarf musician appeared who played an incredible selection of jazz and classical and rock. All the guests wanted to know where Flynn had found this dwarf genius, and in the end he explained: 'I did a good turn for this witch,' he said 'and she said she would give me anything I wanted. The trouble is, she was a bit deaf, and she thought I asked for a twelve-inch pianist.'

The taboo violation involved in producing the second, 'puzzle-answering' signified – 'penis' – across the semantic space of the (crucially) final signifier – 'pianist' – is by far the most powerful element in the joke, but taboo-transgressive language is unlikely to be experienced as funny without the marked misuse the verbal signifying structure – the punning doubling of signifieds. The particular trick of this set-up lies in evading – whilst still implying – the precise word 'pianist' until the end: such jokes will not work effectively if the punchline signifier has been identically produced in the set-up, because its normal signified will already be in the Audience's mind and they will not then produce both this and the second signifier *in the same space*. Freud's explanation of such verbal play as 'permitting' the more energetic transgression may well apply, in terms of the psyche's repressive mechanisms; but the marked mistake creates a *discursive* effect, operating between two (or more) people, not just inside one mind. The formal arrangement of the utterance leads the Audience genuinely to produce double signification – which in this instance includes a 'naughty word' – and the laughter that results from their immediately marking this as erroneous language is received approvingly within the Teller's 'understood intention' to joke, so that (as Chapter 1 suggested) the transgressive utterance is confirmed as discursively valid in this moment. It becomes a mutual, yet tacit, discursive production; while in agreeing that what is 'right' here is also marked as 'wrong', this social intimacy constructs itself as a joint observance of the particular rule that has been affirmed: it is 'wrong' to think 'penis' *in the same way as* it is 'wrong' for one signifier to generate two signifieds. Thus joking establishes a collusive possession of the capacity to define that particular rule of usage as the observance of 'proper' – symbolically effective – language.

A weak punch-line joke may insist too much on the fact that a linguistic transgression is being evoked from the Audience, supplying too little structure in which the cognitive 'rightness' holds the transgression(s) in balance. 'Pure' puns traditionally evoke a groan rather than a laugh, a conventional expression of the unease created when the Audience's transgression is not cognitively justified for them. For example, in the old chestnut 'What's black and white and red all over?' the punch-line answer 'A newspaper' indeed gives a doubled signified to the (sound of) the signifier 'red'; but the colour reference is completely eliminated by reinterpreting it (to make sense of the question) as the verb: 'read'. More importantly, the epithet 'laboured', often applied to weak puns, suggests the Audience's ensuing sensation of working to solve the puzzle, with its resultant Symbolic error but without the reward of fully mastering the Symbolic (because the joking intention is not properly operated to confirm the error as a collusively produced meaning). The Audience have been tricked into a transgression in which the Teller does not really share, for the answer implies that the Teller was operating a monistically 'proper' language all along. (Such naked puns, along with those which close 'Shaggy Dog' stories without cognitively justifying their long preamble, are amongst the category of 'anti-jokes' which are actually an aggression against the Audience, no matter how playfully offered.) Weak puns which involve taboo transgression are rather more satisfactory because they implicate the Teller in transgression, as well as offering some Imaginary play to the Audience: 'Why did the sea blush? Because it saw the [avoiding repetition of the identical signifier] ocean's bottom.'

Wherever it operates as a marked Symbolic error, punning – one signifier distinctly producing two signifieds – is an easily identified mechanism which forms a basic 'building block' of joking. Operating in verbal language, it has the recognition of a name and can be identified in visual as well as verbal joking: I have already suggested that many gags, epitomised by our old friend 'the man who slips on a banana skin', can be described as the rapidly doubled production of two conceptualisations (basically competent/incompetent) on one semantic site. Whereas the mechanism of verbal joking elicits its Audience's transgression by making this the necessary solution to some sort of puzzle, visual joking usually depends upon action arranged so that the incompatible signifiers are produced in very rapid succession – one reason why slipping is likely to be a funny spectacle is the speed with which the victim is translated from competence to its opposite. Laughter at visual jokes is usually produced immediately, whereas verbal jokes may be followed by several silent seconds in which the Audience works out the puzzle.

Punning, however, is one particular version of a wider operation in which a cluster of excessive, contradictory significations are evoked, which are all in some way valid, but cannot all be 'properly' fitted at the same time to the signifying event. Thus – although there may not be one particular point which on its own carries specifically doubled signification – the utterance is constructed so that it cannot make sense *without* holding, across some single point, two understandings which are *structurally* incompatible. The mechanism could be labelled, in the logician's terminology, 'equivocation', and its specific error-triggering operation can be identified in both verbal and visual structures. A television commercial for 'Hamlet' cigars (screened in spring 1991) comically extolled their soothing qualities by showing a man who is rendered serene by smoking one, despite a horde of monkeys immobilising his car in a safari park. The best joke is that the monkeys jack the car up and take off its wheels. This is not strictly a pun, but a double or equivocal set of signifieds is produced because the monkeys' behaviour is destructively mischievous – which monkeys really can be – and taking off a car's wheels is indeed destructively malicious; but (since monkeys are actually unable to jack up a car) it is 'improper' to hold the sense of 'monkeys' and that of 'stealing car wheels' together on the site of destructive mischief. Yet making sense of the advertisement's utterance requires us to do just that: a breach of the Law at the level of 'one construction per perception' rather than, strictly, 'one signified per signifier'.

To tease the mechanism out in even more detail, the solemnly methodical effort of the apes' demolition – including deliciously plausible shots of the jack being swiftly and efficiently pumped up – produces sliding doublings of 'orderly' and 'disorderly' behaviour, and of the socially coded values 'work = good energy' conjoined with 'aggression = bad energy' – which would be funny without the additional equivocation of applying these to non-human destructiveness. Similar doublings are involved, for example, in the sort of sequence where Laurel and Hardy almost ceremoniously, in calm and escalating separated actions, reduce each other's car to smithereens. The imaginatively enjoyed, permitted/forbidden violence is made fully 'joking' (and so very funny) through the equivocal constructions which are incited.

Many verbal jokes also turn on an operation of equivocation rather than strict punning. It is, for example, the mechanism of a joke which entails a wine connoisseur loudly complaining in a restaurant that successively offered bottles are the product of a different château, slope of the vineyard, and then year from those he ordered; finally an infuriated fellow customer who is drunk (the superficially rationalising explanation of much implausible behaviour in joking) hands him a glass to taste. The connoisseur spits it out, saying, 'This is piss'. 'I know,' says the drunk, 'but how old am I?' Elements at work here include the taboo breach of mentioning urine and degrading the power-claim of wine connoisseurs, which we construct as illegitimate if we label it snobbish; but the Symbolic transgression that constitutes these as joking is the equivocation of rational 'telling wine's age by tasting it' and irrational 'telling a person's age by tasting their bodily fluid'.

Within my overall argument that joking's valence springs from its psychically charged violation of Symbolic Law, the mechanisms I am identifying here are largely compatible with 'incongruity' theories of laughter which have been sketched – and sometimes worked through in diagrammatic detail – at least since the Scottish philosopher Beattie, in 1776, observed that it arose 'from the view of two or more inconsistent, unsuitable or incongruous parts or circumstances, considered as united in one complex object or assemblage' (quoted in Howarth, p. 13). Arthur Koestler and, more recently, Walter Nash (in relation to verbal joking) and Jerry Palmer (in relation to comic film) detail mechanisms that could be described, in my own terminology, as generating doubled signification, though without fully exploring joking's second, marking, phase. The danger in any unifying definition of the mechanisms of joking is that these may be taken as a single, reductive 'explanation' of what is always so heavily overdetermined. The advantage is the emphatic focus upon the language operation as what defines joking.

A joke like 'Errol Flynn' is typical of socially exchanged jokes in involving some taboo reference, but making this acceptable because it is produced on the back of verbal manipulation which 'permits' it cognitively (it 'makes sense') as well as (in Freud's model) psychically. Producing tabooed words and thoughts can thus be seen as a separate element of Imaginary pleasure which enhances the potency of often minimal Symbolic manipulations. In the context of joking usages, however, taboo systems can themselves be identified as linguistic structures, albeit simple ones, wherein words, actions and objects function to carry the significations 'clean/dirty' or 'permitted/forbidden'. The elements comprising such structures do not fully satisfy Saussure's definition of signs as conjoining a signifier and a separable signified: 'snot', for example, does not *represent* dirtiness – rather, 'dirtiness' is a significance accorded, over and above any 'objective' material observation of its physical nature, to the substance: in our hierarchy of bodily excretions, snot does not represent but *is* 'mildly dirty', while tears are 'clean' and faeces are 'very dirty'. As Mary Douglas points out in *Purity and Danger*, such categorisations are wholly prior to facts about germs and infection, appearing in varying forms in all cultures and understandable as systems for 'making sense' of the world.

This returns us to the sense of language as structures whose elements can 're-present' each other that I identified in Lévi-Strauss's work. Prohibitive taboos constitute linguistic systems comprising two mutually exclusive terms – fundamentally: permitted/forbidden – articulated across the hierarchies of elements recognised as involved with them. The joking that leads us momentarily to hold in mind anything that is recognised as 'forbidden' as, simultaneously, 'permitted' can thus be seen to involve a further layer of marked Symbolic transgression, as well as permitted Imaginary play: two incompatible signifiers are again produced across one semantic space. A separate linguistic justification is not always necessary to such joking; small children (and certain adults in certain moods) will find merely *saying* forbidden things funny, when their prohibition is marked and yet the situation is such as to 'allow' them. The same words will not be funny, of course, where no prohibition is marked (a medical lecture, say): it is the recognised violation involved, not (for most people) thinking about 'a penis' *per se*, that creates pleasure in the 'Errol Flynn' joke.

More useful than a distinction between linguistic transgression and taboo violation in joking is the distinction between all the marked Symbolic 'errors' which the Audience is actually incited to produce, and breaches of taboo observance visited upon Butts; the pleasure in the latter instances seems to spring more from the 'forbidden/permitted' expression of hostility (as a recognised Symbolic breach) than from an Imaginary experience of prohibited activity – as in the 'connoisseur' joke, where the urine is funny because a man has been (imagined as) drinking it, rather than because we enjoy thinking about the substance. I shall discuss Butts further in Chapters 3 and 7, but there seems to be a strong urge to express hostility in general, apart from selecting specific targets. The wine-taster may invite his comeuppance by being aggressively snobbish, but he remains a very vague figure. Jokes like 'Why did the monkey fall out of the tree? Because it was dead' are funny (if only when they are told in propitious circumstances) largely through a 'pure', totally untargeted equivocation of aggression (this example is also, perhaps, a 'nonsense' joke – see below).

A great deal of visual joking is, of course (like the banana-skin-slipping man), concerned with visiting unpleasant circumstances on performing targets in ways that produce an equivocally, momentarily permitted expression of hostility, as well as the transgressive doubling of their signification (e.g. 'competent' and 'incompetent') that I have already mentioned.

In verbal joking, an evocation of the sexual act will also be intrinsically funny – as in the joke about 'the honeymoon couple' who 'had terrible trouble because they mistook the Superglue for Vaseline'. The funniness is not, I think, formed simply through permitting a forbidden term, but in the public 'performance' of an imaginary copulation which the received laughter establishes between Teller and Audience. If the Teller completes the joke by pausing and then adding 'all their furniture fell apart' – implying that we were 'supposed' to imagine the Vaseline being employed in place of glue, and not vice versa – that transgressively public imagination is further marked in a context which becomes an anti-joke, provoking the Audience by *denying* that their transgressive solution to the joke's enigma has discursive validity as a 'proper' response.

In Chapter 1, stressing the necessity of understanding the 'intention to joke' for the creation of the full process of discursive exchange which actually constitutes joking, I distinguished an Audience's recognition that an utterance is intended as a joke from its evoking funniness. On the one hand, we may (rightly or wrongly) assume that something we find funny was not offered as a joke. (We may find this *more* funny than if it were taken as an intentional joke, because our discursive competence has been so strongly, autonomously, confirmed.) On the other hand, we may well recognise that an utterance is intended as a joke but not find it funny because its mechanism does not produce a mental response that involves any Symbolic error, or because the implied error is not 'permitted'. Again, the multiplicity of conditions in which joking occurs produces a multiplicity of unpermitting possibilities: our sense of social etiquette may dictate that this is the wrong occasion for any joke, a given target may not be acceptable to us as such, and a taboo whose violation the joke involves may be too strongly internalised for its inhibition to be overcome, or too weakly internalised for breaching it to register as transgressive. In this chapter I am stressing that where an utterance is recognisable as 'a joke' (whether or not we accept the invitation to join in the joking exchange), it is because some element of Symbolic error is intrinsically involved in our making sense of it. A strong mechanism that produces, for example, multiple significations as each fully justified can make us laugh, sometimes to our chagrin, even when we do not want to degrade the joke's target; just as a weak mechanism may move laughter against targets that we do want to degrade, but its presence still makes the difference between 'a joke' and pure aggression.

In formalised jokes (utterances that can objectively be identified as 'a joke' in separation from their occurrence in particular circumstances) the Symbolic error is very often an excess of signifieds, either verbal or (especially in visual joking) conceptual. When they include a doubled production of taboo codings, formal jokes usually incite it *via* this kind of structural excess because, as a wholly separate category, to 'allow' behaviour we simultaneously recognise as 'prohibited' we must be engaged in thinking about the behaviour. Drama or literature can provide an imaginative equivalent of our engagement with actual events, but formal jokes are usually too thin to provoke a deeper engagement with events than their immediate formulation. However, what may be thought of as a third category of excess signification can often be found in formal jokes: in the same way that taboo transgressions produce a thought or an imagined action as at once 'permitted' and 'forbidden', in these jokes the evoked transgression is a doubled evaluation of an action as 'rational/irrational'. This is a very fundamental joking mechanism (and I shall return to it, and the groups it conventionally targets, in Chapter 7) because the mastery it constructs for jokers is the capacity to think ratio-nally, to be part of the community which is fully subjected within the Symbolic.

The original 'light bulb' joke is a good example: 'How many Irishmen does it take to change a light bulb? Three – one to hold the bulb and two to turn the table.' I think only

familiarity can prevent anyone finding this very funny (if we
allow that it has no application to real Irish people).[2] The
action of the two men 'turning a table' presents an initial
puzzle of which the Audience are incited to make sense.
'Turning the table' does, on reflection, make perfect sense
because this turns the third man, and so his hand, which is
holding the bulb that needs to be turned to fit into the socket;
but the action is also absurdly excessive (since he needs only
to wiggle his wrist). As a method of 'changing a light bulb' the
activity the joke leads us to imagine is at once perfectly
rational and completely irrational, and we are held in absolute
oscillation between the two constructions.

Visual gags can operate in the same way. The famous scene
in which Basil Fawlty 'beats up' a car that has broken down
when he urgently needed it ('Gourmet Night' in the first series
of *Fawlty Towers*: Cleese and Booth, pp. 129–30) has many
joking pleasures, including our imaginative enjoyment of a
pure aggression-taboo transgression deliciously 'displaced' on
to the 'faulty' character; but its primary mechanism is an
equivocation – not of different significations, but of the
activity as simultaneously 'rational' (when someone deliberately thwarts you, you want to beat them) and (since cars have
neither volition nor feeling) 'irrational'.

The episode 'Communication Problems' from the second
series of *Fawlty Towers* offers an example of a situation that is
often contrived in comedies to suspend the Audience at length
between 'rational' and 'irrational' constructions: a guest, who
is both tetchy and deaf, is trying to instruct Manuel, the
Spanish waiter, to confirm her reservation. Baffled by her
English, he responds:

> MANUEL: Que?
> MRS RICHARDS: . . . What?
> MANUEL: . . . Que?
> MRS RICHARDS: K?
> MANUEL: Si.
> MRS RICHARDS: C? (*Manuel nods*) KC? (*Manuel looks
>   puzzled*) KC? What are you trying to say?
> MANUEL: No, no – Que – What?
> MRS RICHARDS: K – what?

MANUEL: Si! Que – what?
MRS RICHARDS: C.K. Watt?
MANUEL: . . . yes.
MRS RICHARDS: Who is C.K. Watt?
MANUEL: Que?
MRS RICHARDS: Is it the manager, Mr. Watt?
MANUEL: Oh, manager!
MRS RICHARDS: He *is.*
MANUEL: Ah . . . . Mr. Fawlty.
MRS RICHARDS: What?
MANUEL: Fawlty.
[. . .]
MRS RICHARDS: Fawlty? What's wrong with him?

What the two characters say is perfectly rational, given what each *understand*s the other to be saying; but Manuel and Mrs Richards's *mis*-understand each other without realising it. The Audience are presented with a perfectly rational conversation, in that each response is a sensible reply to what the speaker thinks the other has said, which is simultaneously completely irrational, in that no mutually understood meaning is being constructed. This frequently represented kind of 'logical-but-meaningless' exchange, produced by mistakenly understood intentions, can generate the kind of laughter that hurts your ribs, because its suspension in a 'rational but irrational' reading can be considerably sustained.

A particular version which goes back at least as far as Plautus, who probably borrowed it from an earlier Greek script, is produced by plotting twins, assumed to be indistin-guishable. (Shakespeare borrows the idea several times, while Dario Fo up-dates it in *Trumpets and Raspberries*, where two men's identical appearance results from a plastic surgeon's mistake.) Scenes are generated in which, for example, a wife 'rationally' berates her husband, who is refusing to recognise her, while (in what is in fact the same conversation) a man 'rationally' tries to escape a strange woman who is claiming that he is married to her. In this sort of scene the *characters* may be produced as 'objects' of laughter as they grow irate or frantic, trying and failing to be effective in their world, but the basic mechanism of 'improper rationality' is different from the 'improper behaviour' constructed through 'faulty' comedy characters. The object of laughter is primarily the Symbolic Law which the textual discourse as a whole incites the Audience to break.

Manuel and Mrs Richards, or the twin husband and wife, are being neither stupid nor wilfully taboo-breaking, and the Audience's response is not primarily to do with enjoyment and disavowal of the characters' transgressions; the importantly funny errors are not on stage, but only in the Audience's mind. Whether or not it targets either fictional or actual people, it is not the aggression of Butts but the *'ab-use'* of language which constitutes joking.

All joking thus depends upon our paying attention to our own activity of signification. As I suggested above, when actual events appear funny to us we have become suspended – though not usually consciously – in our doubled and so transgressive signification of the action to ourselves, and all joking appears to depend upon unusual attention to how an utterance is articulated, rather than to its contents.

Direct attention to the form of any utterance implies our awareness (at some level) of the fact of signification as distinct from the extra-linguistic effect the utterance involves – its reference to and intended influence on what is outside its signifying structure. Attending to its form creates the signifier as excessive to its signified, producing an evident gap in the 'clipping' of the two that constitutes 'a sign' (so that an excess of the signifier is in itself a breach of language's basic rule of ratio). As this will be one part of all joking's effect, so, vice versa, drawing attention to 'the fact of signification' by some excess in the content or delivery will make any utterance joking – if that intention is understood. For example, the mild and unoriginal irony involved in a damply smiling 'Lovely weather!' when we encounter someone in a downpour has the effect of slightly rearranging the 'dictionary' signifier–signified relationship. In understanding 'lovely' to designate its opposite, speaker and hearer have shared and mutually marked a tiny linguistic transgression, and in thus paying attention to the form of their exchange it is rendered very slightly joking. The main effect and intention of this sort of exchange is to affirm friendliness by mobilising the social intimacy that the Teller–Audience relationship always constructs.

Irony is not usually very funny, since while it reverses and so advertises the conventional designations of terms, it leaves the rule of ratio intact. More comical is the use of vocabulary and delivery which entails reference to modes of discourse other than that which would be transparently 'normal' in the context: something is said or done in a manner which registers as intentionally excessive to the situation – 'too much' emotion or 'too high/low' a diction. At the same time – or separably – the speech or action is understood as a 'negative quotation', referencing how some other individual or group (here operating as a Butt) would utter.[3]

If a text's excess is 'marked' as funny, the language has been disavowed, not identified with. What we laugh 'at' in the case of an apparently serious text which has failed to implicate us for some reason is very similar to what we are likely to laugh 'with' in joking texts; but while laughing 'at' the serious text implies laughing at its 'inept' authorial speaker, in response to joking we accept the invitation to identify with the 'author ego'; we construct a 'proper' language in which it speaks 'for' us, even though the text is marked as 'improperly' excessive, because the language is constructed not directly as 'the author's' but as negatively quoted.

Again, this is most easily recognisable in mildly joking social exchange whose primary aim is to create intimacy rather than considerable funniness: we may use a slightly slang phrase, or a line from some current advertisement, to greet someone when we want to establish our friendliness towards them. It is 'friendly' (of course) because it is slightly joking, and it is slightly joking because it involves an excess of signifier which mildly transgresses the law of language. The centrality of the full discursive exchange within an understood joking intention, so that the Symbolic transgression is collusively marked via the received response, may be uncomfortably demonstrated in this sort of social exchange when the Audience fail to recognise that your aberrant diction is intentional (they may think you 'know no better' than to use a slang phrase). Any joking – 'negative' – quotation similarly, obviously, depends delicately upon not only mutual recognition but mutual evaluation of the source.

The aspect of such parody which it is useful to note at the
moment is its operation as 'joking' between Teller and
Audience (apart from their excluding 'degradation' of a
source), in functioning to mark 'the fact of signification' by
advertising the signification's form. This is an element in most
joking texts where, since they are more complex and more
funny than most social exchange, the signification often
appears to be multiplexly interleaved with other devices that
can be analysed separately. In all these cases we can identify a
self-advertising excess of signification, which may not involve
a punning/equivocation proliferation of signifiers, but still in
itself satisfies the criterion of markedly breaching the Symbolic
Law.

Texts may thus jokingly refer to others' discourse, without
emphatically treating them pejoratively; they may be *self-*
referential, jokingly drawing attention to any one of the
signifying structures they themselves involve; or they may
exhibit, like 'nonsense' jokes, the fundamental structure of
signification.

Any collection of 'parodies' will exhibit many examples of
the first, where an author's style is recognisably reproduced
but not deeply scorned. Styles – and the signifying system
they entail – can also be parodied where no particular speaker
is implied. For example, television comedy shows in the 1980s
were full of sketches where the grave vocal mannerisms
associated in general with newscasters and the presentation of
current affairs programmes were employed to deliver trivial or
absurd material ('To discuss this vital issue we have in the
studio Professor Peterson of Manchester University and a
small rock'). One element that made such sketches funny was
their foregrounding of a signifying system that has now
become recognisable, where voice tone and emphasis designate any verbal content as 'important'. Much literary joking
depends, of course, on using a style that is markedly excessive
to its material – too lofty or too passionate – without implying
a specific target 'who talks like this'. In drama the acting style
as well as the words can be self-advertisingly funny in this
way: the stylised gestures of melodrama, which were read
transparently in nineteenth-century theatre and in early film as
appropriate significations of emotion, today appear 'unnatural'

and excessive, and so produce laughter. Any convention of emotional effect, in fact, will be funny when it is registered, as Mel Brooks's films (*Airplane, Blazing Saddles*) constitute compendia of devices whose repetition has made them into jokably recognisable clichés.

When such stylistic advertising is employed within a narrative it functions as self-reference as well as parody, because the Audience's attention is drawn to 'the fact' of the text they are engaged with, as well as to other, external significations. In the last episode of a BBC situation comedy called *Sorry!* the weedy hero finally escaped from his fearsome and overpossessive mother's house. Playing with the possibility of mixing serious with comic effect, a close-up of the mother's face showed her sad expression as his removal van drew out of the drive and the kind of music usually employed to colour such moments welled up. That screen cliché was indexed when mother yelled 'Turn that off!' and produced silence – mother had behaved with her characteristic, comic belligerence, but towards something that was part of the language constructing 'her'; and so the 'language' of television was advertised. Here the fictional surface was reconstituted by cutting to a shot of a chagrined neighbour who had just – as we now 'read' – switched off his car radio.

If the fictional surface is not recuperated, the joking effect of material self-reference tends towards what is often labelled 'surreal' – in terms of linguistic manipulation, towards the foregrounding investigation of signification's fundamental operations. An early *Monty Python* sketch operated not dissimilarly from the gag in *Sorry!*, but with a potentially more disquieting effect, when a group of men found themselves trapped in a room because 'everywhere outside is on film'. As they tried to leave through the doors and then through the windows, studio interior shots (on video) cut to external shots of their trying to exit and retreating, which were precisely 'on film'. The 'linguistic' convention that 'film represents outside, video inside' is indexed and so comically excessive, but here there is no recuperation to the dependability of technical language elements operating significantly.

The obvious examples of the *self*-reference of texts are when they speak of themselves as entities within the world they describe. This is jokingly transgressive to the extent that it puts strain upon the conventions through which non-joking effects are being created in the text – as the appearance of the first half of the book (as a volume read by the characters) in the second part of Don Quixote's adventures at least troubles our potential emotional engagement with the knight. The appearance of the text 'within itself', of course, functions to advertise to us the fact that we are 'reading', engaged in the fact of signification; direct address to the Audience has the same effect and is, similarly, transgressively joking when it disturbs other effects. Theatre audiences who accepted the 'aside' did not find it disruptive or funny, but those who expect a 'fourth wall' convention, such that the characters have no awareness of the audience, will. From Tudor moralities through Shakespeare's Bottom to modern pantomime, we see dramatists 'playing' with the possibilities of address to the audience originating from 'a character' or from the out-of-character 'performer' – of setting up and then breaking conventions of interpretation. In the right circumstances it can be as funny for us to be forced into public acknowledgement that we are engaged in interpreting a play's action as it is to acknowledge (in the 'Superglue' joke) that we are imagining copulation.

The narrator of a novel may address us without disrupting our 'transparent' interpretation of its fiction, as long as the 'voice' attends to the action at a uniform level of significance (Thackeray, for example, constantly addresses his readers directly, but we hardly notice this, for he comments upon the fictional action as if it were real and important). Sterne's constant direct address to the reader of Tristram Shandy is funny partly because the focus of importance is often suddenly shifted (after a long explanation of why the autobiography itself must be so long, the question 'will this be good for your worships' eyes?' p. 286); and – again partly – because, as in this example, the physical fact of (literally) 'reading' is indexed. Similarly, Jane Austen, towards the end of Northanger Abbey, tells her readers that they must already have realised that the characters' problems are about to be solved because of 'the tell-tale compression of the pages before them' (Oxford Classics edition, p. 270). The transgressively advertised language is not the physical act, in itself, of looking at marks on paper, but the conventional signifying structure whereby an authorial voice is understood to 'speak' to us, retelling the narrative which it is perfectly possible to create from several temporal positions at once (as, in the extreme, in *Wuthering Heights*); what Sterne and Austen jokingly call to our awareness is that our own moment of reading is of a wholly separate order, and that all the fictional time is mentally created by us through our physiological manipulation of the pages of the material book.

Joking which foregrounds and so questions the very structures on which the text's capacity to signify is grounded can be described as 'non-sense' joking. Where 'Irish'-type jokes create an equivocation of action or speech as 'rational/irrational', non-sense creates the equivocation that utterance is or is not 'significant' in any way: that it is, or is not, language-as-such. The most obvious examples are productions of verbal language – for example poems by Lewis Carroll or Edward Lear, where what are apparently 'proper' sentences containing 'proper' words are not – quite – sensible: the 'form' of verbal language is indexed by these instances which resemble it in every respect except that of effective designation; for example, the fatal problem en-countered in Carroll's 'Hunting of the Snark'.

> In the midst of the word he was trying to say,
> In the midst of his laughter and glee,
> He was suddenly, silently, taken away,
> For the Snark *was* a Boojum, you see.

This is one element in screen jokes, like the Python 'on film' gag (the switch from video to cine film should but does not carry significance) or the Laurel and Hardy sequence where an initial shot shows Laurel shouldering the front of a long plank and a set of shots of the plank going past the camera ends with Laurel again, holding the back end. The language of film editing, which we mobilise to 'read' a consistent pre-camera reality from a series of edits, has been efficiently followed only to produce an impossibility. When Harpo Marx produces sudden and 'pointless' activity – like whipping out a pair of scissors and cutting off a stranger's tie – I think the wondrous pleasure stems not only from a suddenly 'permitted' imaginary aggression but also from our recognition that the activity of

signification, which joking affirms through its marked transgression, is here totally emptied of content: we have the form
of a joke, but the answer to the 'puzzle' is that there is no
'answer'. There is no reason for the action, and we notice our
own activity of 'making sense' in trying to operate it on a site
that invites, but finally refuses it. Thus what is advertised and
made jokingly excessive is not merely filmic convention, but
language-as-such.

'Excess signifier' mechanisms are thus diverse and often
subtly interwoven with other joking operations, but this is not
the only reason why their discussion is more complex than
that of 'excess signifieds'. Although excess production of
signifieds will usually be involved with non-joking effects in
its mobilisation of Imaginary pleasures, and although Imaginary
operations are in tension with the Symbolic Law's constitution
as a primary repression, at the level of conscious discourse it is
not difficult to sort the proliferating elements back into
'properly' distributed signs: that is to say, prohibitive taboos
that are violated can usually be easily recognised, while puns
and equivocations can be rationally explained, even though
particular instances usually involve more effects than their
central, 'doubling' mechanism. It is fairly easy to state the
'proper' usage which the excess signified negotiates. A marked
excess of signifier can often be seen as operating quite simply
to create an utterance as joking, yet when we come to pursue
the possibilities of such disrupted language we find that the
non-comic pleasures and disturbances which are deeply
associated with the proliferation of language form are less easy
to recuperate. It is less easy to construct the 'proper' usage
which such joking violates and affirms. At its extreme, it is not
our hold on Symbolic agency but the validity of Symbolic
agency itself which is troubled by the proliferation of
signifiers – it does not so much index the difficulty as question
the possibility of 'making sense'.

Joking of some kind appears as a necessary exercise for all
language-users to test and confirm their control in the
Symbolic Order. Small children and even apes taught to hand-
sign language apparently begin to joke as soon as they reach
Symbolic competence.[4] As we grow older, what we enjoy
joking about and what kind of joking we enjoy becomes more

diverse. Perhaps the more our self-construction becomes involved with Symbolic competence, the more we are likely to enjoy joking which is *wholly* about language. Jokes that are totally 'non-sense' – dealing, I think, with the fundamental operation of signification as such – are disliked (not found funny) by many people. I like them, and see in them the epitome of the joking form. I am thinking of jokes such as Harpo's tie-cutting or – an example given by Freud – the man in a restaurant who 'dips his hands in the mayonnaise and seeing the other customers' horrified looks seems to notice his mistake and apologises: "I'm so sorry, I thought it was spinach" '. As Freud expounds: 'these extreme examples have an effect because they rouse the expectation of a joke, so that one tries to find a concealed sense behind the nonsense. But one finds none: they really are nonsense' (1905, pp. 138–9). Freud dismisses these as 'a take-in', anti-jokes that provoke the Audience. If, though, such a joke is genuinely enjoyed, Teller and Audience have confirmed together their capacity totally to manipulate language, mutually transgressing its most fundamental rule that sense be made, and affirming jointly their discursive capacity to found signification upon their recognition that all 'meaning' is arbitrary, but real [*sic*] because we *do* the act.

Whatever 'sense' or 'truth' a joke may conceal, however, whatever targets and taboos it allows us to attack, however many layers of effects it entails, all joking discourse can be seen to include an 'ab-use' of language through whose exchanged marking we claim mastery of Symbolic competence.

Notes

1. See *Jokes and their Relation to the Unconscious*, Chapter 3.
2. The construction of 'conventional Butts' is examined in Chapter 7.
3. Negative quotation says that 'someone else – ineptly – speaks like this', and it is, of course, constantly employed in comic texts. This is most obvious when the 'improper' language is put into the mouth of a character, but the authorial diction of joking texts – literary or performative – can also function in this way.

   A construction of 'negative quotation' often, however, alternates with or slides through nuances amongst directly received 'proper' language; i.e. joking and poetic understandings of formally excessive discourse are poles of possibility. The joking marking can be minimal (as in most responses to Austen); or what is marked as comically excessive can at the same time (in practice, I think, in very rapid alternation) be 'mixed' with affective implication (the response twentieth-century comedy has often played on, from Chaplin through *Steptoe and Son* and later situation comedies). It is also possible for the excess to be marked as a linguistic misuse, but not as truly transgressive because it is constructed as creating 'poetic' significance – which produces versions of 'ambiguity' readings in, for example, Metaphysical poetry's 'Wit' as well as Modernist texts. It is always possible for what is fully funny also to signify, in a total textual context, an implicating assertion (e.g. in 'satire' as defined in Chapter 6).

Literary texts can offer their language as joking very obviously through a separation of 'enunciator' and 'enunciated', a technical distinction which in turn can be identified most clearly in joking texts. George Grossmith's novel *The Diary of a Nobody* is narrated in the first person by its 'hero', Mr Pooter, who is clearly established as unable to behave/think/speak in 'proper' language (through the kind of cumulative detail indicated on pp. 78ff. – for example, the disproportion and powerlessness of his behaviour). When Pooter celebrates his discovery of 'enamel paint' or ends his account of crude party games with his 'how we did laugh', the audience is invited to laugh 'with' the (constructed) author as a 'proper' speaker who marks all Pooter's language as 'inept'.

With more complexity, Voltaire produces Pangloss's optimistic 'this is the best of possible worlds' – an absurd response, given the hideous and taboo-transgressive harm the characters in *Candide* suffer – as fatalistic: a mistake finally transmuted into an understanding acceptance. Jane Austen opens *Persuasion* with a description of the well-descended 'Sir Walter Elliot', who 'never took up any book but the Baronetage' because 'there he found . . . any unwelcome sensations arising from domestic affairs changed naturally into pity and contempt as he turned over the almost endless creations of the last century (p. 1).' The language here is 'dialogic' in the way that Peter Womack applies the term to Dickens's repeated use of the word 'magnificence' in describing Sir Leicester Deadlock (*Bleak House*, Penguin edition, 1971, pp. 452–3; Womack, p. 8).

These examples illustrate a sliding from the distinctness of joking intention in Grossmith, through Voltaire's broad comedy –

his characters are considerably 'degraded', which simultaneously carries manifest 'serious' intention – to the half-smile Austen raises at the expense of Sir Walter. Neither Austen nor Dickens is directly 'quoting' their character; we (are invited to) recognise the relative valuations of 'domestic affairs' and ancient aristocratic lineage as Sir Walter's, marked as ineptly exaggerated between author and reader; Deadlock's 'magnificence' (e.g. 'Not a little more magnificence, therefore, on the part of Sir Leicester') is located even more precariously. In Womack's words: 'the narrator has, as it were, found the term . . . in the vocabulary of . . . some uncritical admirer of the aristocratic values he represents . . . but he is using it without conviction and getting it slightly wrong' (p. 8).

The degree of marked 'wrongness' controls the extent of funniness, while – as Chapter 6 explores – other distinctions amongst negatively quoted language can be made in respect of how clearly the 'wrong speaker' is located as actually existing outside the text, and the gravity of what is 'wrong' – so that terms such as 'parody' and 'satire' can be more precisely defined. Gerald Mast (p. 5) identifies 'parody' as one of his eight 'comic structures', but since it is a form of quotation, it often appears as local and sometimes as evanescent moments within texts, rather than as an overall structure.

4. For children's joking, see McGhee and Chapman (1980), e.g. pp. 59–90, 213–36; for apes', see McGhee (1979), ch. 3, *passim*.

3

The Butt
The Third Position

The 'third position' this chapter discusses is that of the 'Butt', which is constituted by the joking exchange as excluded from the Teller–Audience relationship and, in being so, reciprocally confirms the collusion of those two positions as masterful jokers. When it involves actual targets, joking constructs these as *not* fully members of the community of proper speakers, and this involves complex and often strong feelings towards them. The resulting abjection of actual targets in joking forms its most conspicuous and usually debated 'political' effect, and I shall discuss this in Chapter 7; but in this chapter I continue to consider the specifically linguistic aspect of joking, from which its particular and considerable political potency arises.

Given that joking discourse *per se* is identified by its manipulation of language, what is recognisably 'joking' entails our suspension within the fact of signification: when they are funny, actions (enacted or described) are unusually attended to as sites of conceptualisation, just as where 'pure' wordplay raises laughter we are noticing the form of the words before their designation. Understanding the operations of joking involves noticing not only that whatever we think 'about' (whatever is meaningful) is a site *in* language – i.e it can be analysed as a value in a signifying structure – but also that in the event of thinking, our mental contents are sites *of* language, locations of the *activity* which is 'signification', which involve psychic energies as well as abstractable structures. Thus when they are considered as psycholinguistic entities, whatever elements we have in mind appear as multiplex and ambiguous: figures engage us because they are reversible and multivalent sites of feelings that are *rationally* distinct and exclusive – desire and hostility, dependence and fear – because they always entail those Imaginary compressions which the Symbolic Order strives to delimit. An element functioning as a Butt will thus involve powerful 'doubled' relationships at an affective ('emotional') level with the Teller/ Audience, 'joker', group. It is precisely this multiplexity which renders a Butt available and effective as a site of semantic excess, and tracing this is intended to elucidate the unambiguous, material, social effects of joking, not to efface them.

The obvious effect involved in laughing at someone or something is that it has been 'brought low', *de-graded*. Specifically, a Butt can be seen as denied *discursive* potency – the power to be an agent who has intentional effect in the world. Attending so 'someone' as a site of *our* language-making renders them objects of our discourse and denies their own subjectivity as language-makers. To be psychically effective, however, this abjection must follow from the Butt's first being accorded power – Butts are precisely degraded from the power to construct and define *us*, within *their* language-making. Parallels with the Symbolic Law in its aspect of threat appear here: every figure that makes an effective joking target can be found in some way to be (at least at that moment) invested as a projection of the Law which embodies the capacity to 'recognise' our subjectivity and to annihilate us (to 'rule us out') when we transgress its psychically demanding restrictions.

At one level the Symbolic Law is the 'third position' in all joking, and in both parts of the total joking exchange. When the aberrant language-use is incited by the Teller and genuinely produced by the Audience, its power is flouted and it is 'degraded' by the success of that breach. The complete operation of joking further involves the tacitly affirmed correct usage and, therefore, a reinstatement of the Law as the third position through which Teller and Audience construct themselves as subjectively valid. However, the particular targets of joking are not reinstated, because the erroneous usage is displaced on to them. They are constructed as identities who are significantly discursively incompetent, and whose ineptness distinguishes them from us, reinforcing our own identity as fully subjected, 'law-abiding' masters of discourse.

The object of laughter has been made into a joke, and a joke's effects in the world are of no consequence. This is how we identify (or elect) something as a joke; this is demonstrated in social terms by the insult involved in calling anything serious 'a joke'. Precisely the same transgression is involved in treating an utterance as a joke in attending to its linguistic form while disregarding its normal effects. Colloquially, to tell someone 'You must be joking' is a refusal to accept the consequences of their utterance. It is not something you say when you really think someone intends to joke (except as a trenchantly effective way of refusing their offered collusion). Challenging a statement you recognise as seriously intended by saying 'That's a joke' has the same implication as calling a person or their activities 'a joke' – we mean they do not have the effect in the world *that they intend*. Calling something or someone 'a joke' is equivalent to deliberately laughing at them, a *pretence* that you find them funny. This extreme case of deliberate, pretended response exhibits what is crucially occurring when laughter is spontaneous and genuine.

Terms such as 'ridicule' and 'derision' demonstrate that consciously constructing a person as the object of laughter is generally recognised as degrading. Deliberately to laugh at someone may be ghastly, if it is the torturer, or heroic, if it is the victim; but it is always an articulation of contempt. Contempt implies superiority mixed with hostility: while 'pure' hostility might lead to physical fighting or the direct abuse which is its verbal equivalent, contempt refuses to recognise the opponent as an equal worthy of fighting ('Sir, you are not a gentleman') and sneering, jeering – utterances with some admixture of joking – index a commensurate refusal to engage at the level of the opponent. Yet there is an element of attention and effort in these limit instances of deliberately contrived 'laughing at'. We do not bother to pretend to laugh at someone whose actions really have no possible effect upon us. The same is true of spontaneous laughter.

Identifying the object of laughter as 'degraded' points to the *two* affective attributes of the object, in relation to the laugher: 'laughing at' is always aggressive, it 'puts people down' in signalling that they are down-put, but that could not happen unless they were originally perceived as 'up' – as in some way holding power over and thus (by definition) potentially threatening the laugher.

Deliberate laughing is a claim that an offered threat is nugatory, a declaration that 'You thought you had power over me – but you haven't'; or, as the biblical horse in Job 39:25 'saith among the trumpets, Ha, ha!'. Spontaneous laughter always has among its triggering components a *genuine* sense of threat overcome, and being 'half-frightened' is an element in funniness, sometimes a considerable one. A child being tickled by a romping adult exhibits this very clearly. The equations producing the funny balance of rapidly perceived power/not-power are highly varied. As in the case of 'the man who slipped on a banana skin', any person demonstrating competence can be constructed as claiming power and so offering a threat, though of course the more evident the claim to power, the more probable funniness as a response to their mishap. Almost completely to the contrary, someone or something which is normally totally within our power, such as a baby or a kitten, can evoke laughter by apparently claiming power, even the minimal power of 'human competence' – a toddler solemnly hammering pegs with an expression of intense concentration, 'like a grown-up workman', or a kitten pouncing 'like a tiger' will be funny, because we know that the power they momentarily signify has no substance. They will be even funnier if they (for example) fall over during this display of competence, confirming its falseness; and they will stop being funny if they seem to have hurt themselves – as will (usually) the genuinely powerful victim.

The degrading of the comic object almost invariably involves some harm befalling them; but spontaneous (as opposed to deliberate) laughing at people is complicated because in most instances it includes what Jerry Palmer calls 'comic insulation' (p. 45). As Palmer notes, this sense that the victim is 'insulated' from real harm is included as a necessary element in many definitions of the comic. It is useful, however, to disengage these two comic factors: one, that people are laughed at in virtue of being degraded – which is always hostile and often involves their harm – two, that the conditions in which people being harmed provokes laughter are different from those where it does not.

Ghastly actual suffering can be funny, when it can be constructed as helplessness suddenly replacing some threat. The Elizabethans laughed at the agony of men publicly tortured to death, and Charles Dickens noted how the crowds gathered for a public hanging thought the spectacle amusing. Also, many kinds of harm traditionally inflicted on animals clearly involved making them ridiculous – laughing at them. If bears are no longer available for baiting, and tying tin cans to cats' tails is no longer regarded as normal childish mischief, this kind of activity does still happen and even takes new forms: people do put budgies in microwave ovens. Anything, it would seem, capable of carrying some projected identity is capable of supplying pleasure through exercising power over it. Bringing about its harm is, by definition, exercising power over it; and to whatever extent that exercise includes an awareness of *discursive* transgression, it is experienced as funny.

Cruel joking with animals reported in the news is nowadays consensually regarded as horrible, even mentally sick; but its clear continuity with current joking is demonstrated by the fact that it is often received as funny when stand-up comedians describe it. (In a current routine which includes 'Thought my goldfish needed exercising. Threw him on the lawn. Did about thirty press-ups, then gave up', one funny element is the fish's helplessness.) For most people today, actual animals are 'sympathetic', so that seeing them in pain stops us laughing at them. However, the same condition applies to both people and animals: what displays the failure of their 'power' is inherently funny whenever the Audience's disposition to the victim *inhibits empathy* and opens them not simply to hostility but to the degradation of being denied discursive agency; and what establishes such degrading often involves some kind of physical harm (apart, that is, from the mental hurt which is one of its obvious effects). What is degrading emphasises the victims' physical ineffectiveness: they cannot achieve their intended effect in the world (it is more degrading to trip someone than to punch them); and/or, by associating them with taboo activities and substances, emphasises their ineffectiveness as 'proper' people. In extreme instances intense human suffering has even, in recent times, been treated as funny by 'normal' people – it is 'degradation', not just 'punishment', that will be imposed on people who have wielded power as terror: the dictator hung upside down, the collaborators' heads shaven. Bullies, of course, humiliate (not just 'harm') their victims; they demonstrate their power over them by making them 'figures of fun' in situations often reminiscent of the degradations that comic performers enact.

Laughing at the considerable distress of real people is an extreme instance; it does not feel 'happy' and would not be included within the category of 'humour'. Hostile feelings – although they are the reverse of sympathetic feelings – towards a victim mean that the 'audience' *are* implicated in the event and not totally suspended in its linguistic construction. Nevertheless, the line between violence which also humiliates its victim, practical joking, and 'pretended' funny events in texts is a slippery one. It depends upon the relationship between Audience and Butt, not upon the specificities of the action – what is or has been taken to be funny in texts, and what has been done to humiliate in actuality, involve similar or even identical activities. The Ku Klux Klan, for example, began as a boisterous drinking club whose ex-Confederate troopers played 'spooky' practical jokes on all their neighbours. These developed into 'scaring', in particular, newly freed slaves through practical jokes such as offering a false hand to shake, and riding off leaving it in the other's grasp – before, of course, progressing to lynchings (see Wade, pp. 32–7). The 'false-arm' gag in turn appears amongst sixteenth-century commedia dell'arte *lazzi* (Gordon, p. 29). (Webster makes use of a similar false hand to create a non-comic moment of 'terror' in *The Duchess of Malfi*.) Hanging upside down happens to Harold Lloyd, or to the Michael Crawford character in *Some Mothers Do 'Ave 'Em*, as well as deposed dictators.

In texts as in actuality, the more the victim suffers, the more implacably unimplicated an audience has to be to find that funny, even if the 'base level' of acceptable harm is always higher in texts than in actuality. But while considerable suffering can humorously befall characters in distinctly artificial texts such as silent-movie slapstick, or in cartoons,

modern audiences are so trained in reading texts natural-
istically that they may well be moved or disgusted by events that
earlier audiences simply laughed at. The considerable beatings
Molière imitated from commedia dell'arte scenarios are
probably less funny to present-day than to their contemporary
audiences; and we are now a lot less likely to laugh at the
extreme violence – unknowingly eating shit, being urinated on
and similar gruesome happenings – which commedia visited
upon characters with great original comic effect: Mel Gordon
catalogues original commedia routines [*lazzi*] whose violence
and scatology are quite hair-raising to a modern sensibility.
Similarly, in their original reception, many of Shakespeare's
plays – for example, *Twelfth Night*, *The Merchant of Venice* and,
of course, *The Taming of the Shrew* – may have been more
simply funny. Malvolio, Shylock and Kate all strike empathetic
chords now, so that the 'operation of joking' in these texts has
changed (as I shall suggest in the next chapter).

Complexities and contradictions discovered by modern
critics in such plays are not invalidated if they were not
apparent to the original audience; but the difference in
reading does emphasise how important the Audience's
reception is in any formulation of funniness. Laughing at
someone involves our constructing them as discursively
powerful, and then denying them that construction. From
being potent speakers who can confirm or deny our subjectivity, they are changed to impotent figures constructed within
the language exchanged by Teller and Audience.

Suffering itself will be only one element in the complexity of
a situation which evokes funniness, especially within texts.
One other element that very often accompanies it is that
victims struggle against their fate in a flurry of physical or
verbal resistance which reinforces their perceived oscillation
between having and not-having power – i.e. their *degradation*. The proper balance of power/threat – strong enough
to provoke and weak enough to allow degradation, in that
situation – is another.

Figures whose public status gives them institutional power
are obvious candidates for joking objectification. In life, most
groups of people will collude to joke about anyone who holds
power over them as a collective. Children joke about their

teachers, adults joke about their boss. In comedy texts, one
typical figure of fun is a person who exercises public authority.
Texts construct such funny figures in the way we usually need
to think of actual authorities – as illegitimately, and therefore
ineptly, holding their power. When the power – which is
always a threat, just as a threat is always an exercise of power
– is real and immediate, funniness cannot be perceived. As
Plato noted (in *Philebus*), we do not laugh at those who can
retaliate against us. It is funny when someone claiming power
suddenly betrays ineptness which degrades them and removes
their power – a situation comedy texts often supply. In life, by
making jokes we imaginatively supply ourselves the moment
of degradation. Funniness depends upon the almost simultaneous perception of the two states (and thus the operation of
two signifieds in the one semantic space of 'this person').
Similarly, as long as someone is perceived as constantly
'below' us – i.e. degraded in relationship to ourselves – they
are unlikely to be funny.

That last statement may seem obviously inaccurate: surely
there are instances in comedy texts of totally 'put-upon'
victims; in social groups of perennial Butts; and those generic
groups who are the conventional Butts of social and often
textual joking (women, blacks, gays, etc.) are persistently 'low
others' to the joking group. These are three different, 'rule-
proving' exceptions. In comic texts a constant victim will not
be funny unless s/he is also constantly resilient – a particular
instance of the power/no-power *oscillation* which I shall
discuss presently. Similarly, the constant Butt within a local
social group is likely to be 'resilient' in accepting or even
initiating the joking – the effect is to claim a share in the
'Teller' position and thus a measure of power status in the
group. This is the strategy of 'being a clown so they wouldn't
hit me' which comedians tend to claim as part of their
childhood. It operates on the wider, cultural level when
subordinated groups make jokes about themselves (but there is
also often an operation of separately identifying a 'low other'
group within the culturally identified category, from whom the
jokers in turn distinguish themselves, which is exemplified in
German Jews' jokes about 'Ostjuden': Eastern Jews).

Joking about 'low others' is perhaps the clearest exception

which (in the proper sense) proves the rule I am arguing. 'Low others' are a threat to the dominant group that constructs them, because, as I have suggested, there is no point in 'othering' people who have no claim to the identity space you are trying to occupy. Those groups we persistently 'other' are actually those we perceive as very similar to ourselves, but different in one respect – skin colour, reproductive function, accent – which can be fastened on as entailing the low characteristics which make them so 'inferior'. The power/threat they pose is that of escaping this construction, which in consequence needs constant reinforcement. However, although the repetition of conventional joking objects contributes significantly to these social constructions, the energy of individual jokes is not usually derived from hostility to them. In most conventional jokes the Butt stands for 'a stupid person' (who commits a Symbolic mistake without being able to mark it) against whom the Teller/Audience group distinguish themselves (who commit but mark the mistake) as clever, fully human 'masters of language'. What is in each separate instance an individual, psychic empowerment has a communal social effect through stereotype joking's repeated assumption that all members of a conventional target group manifest a particular 'stupid' characteristic.

So all joking objects, the apparently wholly 'low' as well as the evidently 'high', are perceived as holding a power of some kind over the jokers, and it is funny when they are suddenly perceived as not having it. This is funniest when it is the result, as well as the exhibition, of their claimed power being illegitimate. Some kinds of people – above all, women – are constructed as being inherently disqualified from exercising any kind of 'power'. In them any kind of powerful action is illegitimate, threatening, and invites comic degrading. Male comic characters are invested with particular kinds of stupidity – including greed, unreasonable ambition, unsuitable lust – which involve their claiming unjustified power and deliver them to enjoyable humiliation. Such illegitimate power is generally described as a 'fault' and has been constructed, from Plato to Bergson, within a moralistic description of comic effect.

These 'faults' in comic characters have been been defined as 'minor' or 'social' errors, rather than the 'great' faults proper to tragedy, ever since Aristotle's *Poetics*.[1] This can be understood as a reflection of the comic object's construction as 'only language', i.e. as 'a joke' (which Chapter 4 considers), but more simply, what can be taken as a 'minor fault' is 'a-threat-which-can-be-nullified'. The comic object's 'fault' may not consist in doing anything, but only in being a child, or a black, or a woman, who is 'pretending' to full human functioning. Reciprocally, a (perceived) illegitimacy of the object's power-claim – i.e. they are 'faulty' – makes it probable that the Audience will deny them sympathy and find their degradation funny.

However, since the funniness specifically arises through our own transgressive perception of them, it is strictly the signifying Law that is the laughers' object (when two signifieds are constructed across a single semantic space) and only indirectly the target. Not only is no type of event or person 'always and only comic' (as a comparison of serious and comic texts will show), but it is actually the activity of (mis-)using language, not the trigger evoking it, which is funny. Thus laughing at a person enacts the same process as laughing at a verbal utterance, although it can have direct and antagonistic social effects which the 'purely verbal' joke avoids.

Cartoons such as *Tom and Jerry* provide an example of laughing at 'a person' which is free of actual targets, for while the animals are of course 'funny' as projected humans, they do not refer to any conventional categorisation of real people. (Note, however, the maid who occasionally appears from the knees down; since she is a black, and a woman, the power she wields over 'that cat' is inherently comic: it does not frighten *us*, so it is funny that the cat has to be afraid of her. Similarly Spike, the dog with 'Jaws'-type teeth, who terrifies Jerry, has the potential of really frightening the audience diminished by his 'working-class' accent.) We may take such cartoons, then, as a specific illustration of the multiple relationships involved in constructing an object of laughter.

The overt artifice of the cartoon medium is significant in the funniness of cartoons like *Tom and Jerry*, partly because it retards sympathetic 'realis-ation' of the (considerable) harm its victims experience. In fact, cartoons *can* implicate audiences and produce highly affective responses – hands up anyone who did not cry when Dumbo's imprisoned mother rocked him, through prison bars, in her trunk. Perhaps more significantly, though, the total artifice of cartoons allows the textual 'utterance' to be manipulated so as to maximise the audience's 'double-signified' perceptions. That is a simple way of describing what is a very complex practice by which successful comic texts control audience predictions of narrative movement, in the short and long term, so that 'surprising' (i.e. *genuine*) double significations are powerfully elicited. This can happen in a variety of ways, including the carefully suspended satisfaction of expectation: the rock falls on Jerry's head the *third* time he goes through the door, when we had almost forgotten it; as we had almost forgotten *The Alchemist*'s Dapper, gagged with gingerbread in a privy for two Acts, until he shouts for help in the middle of Act V (having eaten through the gingerbread).

Unlike Jonson's comic characters (and many others), Tom and Jerry are never degraded through association with sexual or scatological taboo – such as being locked, specifically, in a privy. Tom and Jerry are made 'dirty', but only with the literal, less psychically charged pollution of mud or tar or soup. As comic objects, then, they suffer degradation by association with 'low' substances and also the terrible (and disempowering) physical harm which the audience is able to 'enjoy', beyond the overtly unreal graphic style of the cartoons, because no one in the cartoon world – including the victim – reacts as if sympathy were appropriate; and also, finally, because the two characters each claim 'faulty power' over the other: the cat wants to eat the mouse, who tries to get him kicked out of the house.

So far I have talked about people being funny in terms of suffering mishaps; but in comedy, characters also act as agents; they cause events as well as suffering them. The element of degradation persists because (a) harm to someone, often themselves, generally results; and (b) what it is funny to *do* involves taboo-breaking. Voluntary taboo-breaking belongs to 'comic heroes' (involuntary taboo *contamination* belongs to 'comic villains'), and involves committing forbidden acts –

sometimes sexual, more often simply aggressive to other people. While we enjoy their 'deserved' harm, there is also an element of identification with transgressive comic characters. This 'identification' is not to do with the realm of affect, of feelings and sympathy. It is to do with constructing people as 'like us' (literally identifying with them) as producers of 'language' – intentions that are effective in the world – that we can share. While in reality the two generally go together, comic response demonstrates that they are separable. We vicariously enjoy 'comic heroes' doing prohibited things that we would like to do ourselves; but even comic heroes rarely get away with their transgressions. The text usually confirms such behaviour is marked as 'wrong' even while we 'enjoy' it (hence its funniness), by visiting the failure of schemes and physical harm upon their perpetrators. The audience can both eat and have their cake; they commit and mark the forbidden actions – as joking's misuse of language is marked while it is committed. There can also be a reversed operation of such identification, in which we experience fear whilst enjoying the negation of its threat. As the powerful villain is degraded, so any threat which is (almost) simultaneously negated creates funniness. This occurs in identification with comic characters – our hero, trapped in a car, balances over a cliff edge – as well as in direct experiences like being tickled.

Identification with comic heroes [sic] is, however, much more obviously through their appropriation of power than their victimisation – and that power is centrally discursive. Comic heroes are conspicuously associated with manipulating discursive conventions to their advantage, and this is importantly, but not definitively, associated with their self-serving manipulations of verbal language: Falstaff, Harlequino and Del Boy (of *Only Fools and Horses*) share the comic hero's capacity to talk themselves out of any corner. Tom and Jerry never speak, but they are constantly tricky, and beyond talking themselves out of difficulties, comic heroes may imaginatively engage Audiences in the experience of escaping conceptual constrictions. They are as 'ingenious' as their representational mode allows: the Pink Panther draws a door to avoid one kind of problem; Basil Fawlty pretends to faint to evade another. There is a distinctive satisfaction when discursive conventions are pre-empted by 'sheer', and usually impossible, physical resistance (a 'Martian' responds to Deputy Dawg's drawn gun by eating it), for if it feels funny, we read this as a triumph of language over the Real. If the 1930s formula 'with one bound Jack was free' strikes us today as *funny*, it is because we mark his escape as discursively and not realistically procured.

Similarly, the cartoon medium also allows Tom and Jerry to display to a high degree one characteristic critics have especially associated with comic *heroism*: after every sequence's flattening, boiling, dismemberment, or whatever, they re-appear inviolate. They suffer constant harm, but as constantly their vitality (in the most literal sense) reasserts itself. Many critics have taken this vicariously enjoyed 'vitality' as the central characteristic of comedy;[2] but although arguments along these lines are amongst those which insist that 'comedy' is not fundamentally located in funniness, effortless resilience is actually likely to be funny, because it is the ultimate 'discursive manipulation'. When such invulnerablity is *not* read as 'language', it is frightening, like the 'Terminators' in the film series. Hammer Horror ghouls were intended to be frightening, but because their technique is now dated (like 'Jack' the 1930s hero), audiences attend to their discursive production and laugh.

As we scrutinise each example of 'someone being funny', we see again how it is the dense and multiple doubling of responses they are eliciting which leads us to laugh at them: pleasurable identification with, and also fear of, power that is awarded and withdrawn – within that attention to the object as a site of language which gives us power over them but, because we use the language transgressively and mark that between us, feels funny.

Notes

1. See, for example, William Howarth's intelligent summary of comic theories (1978, pp. 1–21).
2. E.g. Langer, Torrance, Corrigan – the critics' construction of 'comic vitalism' is examined at length in Chapter 8.

PART TWO

Comedy as Joking Text

Introduction

The word 'comedy' is notoriously difficult to define. All the works examined in this part represent a story which extends across a substantial text – i.e. they go on long enough for discussion of their plot and characters to be sensible; and they demonstrably do so within an 'understood joking intention'. The texts I am considering, then, are narratives which apparently mean to be funny. In exploring how that happens and what effects it has, I shall refine this description to take account of the non-joking elements which appear in many texts that must be included in any sensible definition of the genre; but I shall suggest that it is misleading to identify, as some critics have done, an 'essence of comedy' which is separable from its funniness. In a useful article, Mick Eaton suggests that:

> what remains to designate a product as specifically 'comedy' lies in those excesses – gags, verbal wit, performance skills – which momentarily suspend the narrative. Once again we are back to the tautology, 'it's a comedy because it makes us laugh'. (1981, p. 22)

In agreeing with Eaton's 'tautology', I want to show that the intention advertised by the 'gags . . . [etc.]' contained in most comedies in fact extends the Audience's joking understanding *into* their narrative, whose constituent activities are then given 'unusual attention' in their aspect as language. The defining funniness of comedy, therefore, has effects structurally parallel to but taking a different site from isolated gags, punch-line anecdotes, and so on.

Stories are jokingly represented in novels, to a limited extent in narrative poetry (e.g. Browning's comic monologues) and even in visual art,[1] as well as in dramatic performance; but comedy is overwhelmingly connected with drama, and that is where the focus of this part lies. The word 'drama' means (in Greek) 'the thing done'; thus a story enacted rather than spoken. It is possible to identify many reasons why comedy's joking representation of the world should be most closely associated with dramatic performance.

Performance, first of all, enhances the effects of individual funny moments: because drama's authorial 'Teller' is less immediately present than in literature, the Audience's marking of a transgression (as I discussed in Part One) often feels like a heady self-confirmation of Symbolic mastery – solo laughing – while when other members of a theatre audience laugh too, the correctness of the silent joking response nevertheless finds reinforcement as a proper utterance. Conversely, what is more immediate in drama, the physical presence of represented characters, enhances all the elements of that joking response: we can project our imagined pleasures, and also separate ourselves from the Symbolic violations these entail, more strongly, given the actors there 'before our very eyes'. Again, the Teller's 'absence' helps to suspend the expectation that Symbolic transgressions are going to be provoked, so they are more likely to be genuinely produced; while the overarching 'joking intention', which is usually very clearly signalled, strongly confirms that they *are* discursively valid.

In narrative comedy, though, individual funny moments are not like plums in a serious pudding. They shed their 'flavour' into the whole text; and the more individual jokes are integrated into the story, so that what is funny arises from and furthers the narrative(s), the more we take the total performance as a joking representation. It is through this osmosis of understood intention that the characters' behaviour (which constitutes the story) is then attended to as, in itself, the language of a signifying system – a structure that can be operated properly or improperly, separately from words it may use and from words which may describe it. The medium of performance produces everything it represents, including people speaking, as behaviour – the opposite of literature, which produces everything it represents, including wordless action, as a verbal account. All the enacted behaviour which constitutes a dramatic performance, including speech, can more easily generate interpretative Symbolic encodings which are distinct from verbal language; and this is the second reason why drama is especially apt for presenting stories jokingly.

Verbal language is, of course, an important part of the funniness of comic drama: it presents inept speakers whom the audience laughs 'at' in collusion 'with' the author position, and also witty speakers whom we laugh 'with', whether 'at' other characters or purely 'at' the mastered Symbolic Law; but in a performed narrative the fullest range of 'language' – including all kinds of social codes – is more easily available to attention *as* a signifying system.[2] The second chapter in this part (Chapter 5) is concerned with the specific 'language of exchange' on which comic representations focus their Audiences' attention; Chapter 6 is concerned with the structures and subcategories of the comic genre that then appear. First, however, Chapter 4 examines the moment-by-moment operations of comedy texts which produce a combination of imaginative representation and attention to its signification.

The argument I am making about joking operates in two directions. If what is 'a joke' is definitionally attended to in its aspect as language, then that focus of attention is not being considered as having direct effect in the world – which is 'degrading'. Conversely, in order that anything be 'taken as a joke', awareness of its direct effects in the world must be deferred. When someone in actuality becomes laughable, a combination of circumstances must have occurred in which that is possible; but in comedy texts, characters must be constructed so that an Audience can engage with the action and yet be barred from implication with it. Noticing the mechanisms that make this happen will support my argument that what appears in 'comedy' is not usefully defined as inherently laughable; rather, that these are texts which function 'jokingly', in dynamically *producing* their action in its aspect as language.

Notes

1. Joking intention is involved, for example, in much of Hogarth's work – e.g. the 'Marriage à la Mode' series.
2. Because they are framed together as a 'text', all the elements comprising any performance – its material 'presentation', its suppositional 'representation' and the hermaneutics connecting them – function as a language uniquely constituted on that occasion between the authorial position and the theatre audience. This is another way in which drama especially invites our awareness of our operation as makers of signification, prior to its designating consequences. Foregrounding that awareness produces the 'self-referential' joking which I discussed in Chapter 2. Clearly such joking is entailed with the phenomenon of performance, and its appearance in literature can be discussed in terms of the 'performative' aspects of non-theatrical genres. Like all unusual attention to the fact of signification, it can be manipulated in joking or in other discursive modes, while its more emphatic presence in drama forms another layer of the argument describing why this form of textuality is especially compatible with 'comedy'.

4

Joking Operations of Textual Engagement

If our response to anything taken as 'a joke' involves deferring our attention to its effect in the world, what happens when things are funny can also be described as a lapse of normal implication. So the term 'implication' used in this chapter designates any response which carries some sense of being involved with the effects of an utterance – the precise opposite, in fact, of the response to whatever is taken as a joke. Implication as I am defining it operates in the same way in relation to both social exchanges and texts, but since the contents of texts are totally constructed, an audience's implicated or joking engagement with the action requires specific operations. Funniness is not an inherent characteristic of targets, situations or even utterances, but the effect of attending to 'the fact of signification' within an understood joking intention – an effect some targets, situations and utterances are especially liable to create.

In considering how its presence or absence operates in relation to joking, it is useful to distinguish an affective concern for the persons involved from what I shall call an 'ideological' implication with some kind of value or belief that any utterance may mobilise (although in the last analysis, an engaged response to other people and the mobilisation of value systems cannot be separated). The most obvious way of redescribing affective implication is to say that we sympathise, or even empathise, with the people concerned. In Chapter 3 I noted the frequent observation that such sympathy with a victim precludes our laughing at their misfortunes. I also pointed out, however, that when we see someone as wholly *threatening* to us, they also cannot be the object of our laughter. Thus what are in some ways distinctly different psychic operations – to award sympathy or to yield power – have in common the 'realisation' of their object as an effective entity in our world. The connection then appears between accepting an actual or a fictional 'person' as in this way 'real' (at some level), and accepting that their speaking has real effect in the world. If we respond to an utterance as effective, we are constructing its speaker as a reality in our psychic world, and – vice versa – to those whom we 'realise' we accord the status of 'proper' speakers whose utterances constitute full language, which has reference beyond itself. Hence it is this kind of 'implication' which bars us from taking 'what someone signifies' (in every sense of the phrase) as a joke – while these are of course shifting, dynamic constructions in actuality and in texts.

However we approach actuality, the baseline of the reception of texts is generally established *before* we encounter their action – like all joking discourse, comedies usually carry clear external labels (titles, advertising, etc.) to inform an audience that their predominant intention involves an unimplicated attention. Such reception is also usually encouraged by their content – i.e. the kind of events represented – because in any given culture certain categories of events are strongly connected with dominant, widely implicating valuations; at the moment, for example, interactions that can be constructed as representing 'true love' are very likely to be received seriously. Texts can use these predictable predispositions to move an audience in and out of implication, and the total pre-existing relationship – cultural and personal – between an Audience and the contents of any utterance is always an important determinant of whether or not, in the event, they find it funny. However, there is no content that cannot be presented either jokingly or seriously, if the moment-by-moment details effectively control the audience's implication with it.

The cumulative details of joking texts operate as the reverse of those which attempt to be taken seriously. The latter aim to convince their audiences that within their fictive world a given cause would indeed produce their characters' reactions, so that the characters' joy, suffering, anger, and so on are constructed as realistic. A serious character may well behave 'unreasonably', but there is probably an explanation for this which the audience can accept as in itself realistic, so that the theatre audience is led to construct serious characters as having a psychological complexity. This may then be 'faulty', as Lear's anger with Cordelia can be constructed as his 'madness' – but in according these characters an 'innerness' the audience allows them as amongst the community of significantly 'real' persons; so even if their speaking is muddled or inappropriate, we 'read' it as referring to something beyond itself (i.e their innerness), not as radically – comically – 'improper' language. These are poles of response that can, of course, modulate within a text or even within short sections of it. In *Coronation Street* in summer 1990 Mavis Riley grieved intemperately when her budgie died, and (as this character usually does) that hovered between pathos and comedy; partly because a psychological explanation – that the bird was 'like a child to her' – was offered without being consistently pursued, and partly because there was an oscillation in other characters' response to her misery. The other characters' response is probably the more critical factor in determining how seriously or comically an audience treats represented emotions.

In serious texts, characters behave towards each other as if their behaviour is appropriate, or at least effective. In comedy, they do not. Thus in the opening of *The Alchemist*, when Dol disregards the cause of the men's anger and they ignore her irritation, we have at once a signal and a mechanism which allows their emotions to be read as excessive and as ineffective. Jonson's characters are therefore constructed as 'de-gradable', threatening in their power-seeking over each other but almost simultaneously 'doubled' as powerless: the typical production of the comic object. When Face and Subtle express their rage in whispers because they are, at the same time as being angry, afraid of being overheard, the effect is hugely magnified.

Irritation, since it intrinsically suggests an anger that is both excessive to its object and ineffective in its world, is very likely to be comic; and – other things being equal – anger will be comic if it has either no effect on other characters (as Alf Garnett's wife would ignore his rantings) – which makes the angry character a degraded Butt – or if other characters'

response is an 'unrealistic' fear which constructs *them* as the
degraded Butt, instead of involving the audience with their
suffering. For example, in the situation comedy *'Allo, 'Allo*,
which is set in wartime occupied France, when the Nazi
general roars at his underlings, they shake or make terrified
faces; in reality, and in serious war films, those subjected to
such power would have to hide their fear. Both an absence and
an exaggeration of response construct a character's expressed
anger as not referring to a reality which would implicate the
audience.

Comedy characters' emotional ineffectiveness is, of course,
braided into their discursive ineptness. Whatever kind of
'utterance' they direct to others is inappropriate because it
does not have the effect they intend and/or – vice versa – it
fails in its intention because it is inappropriate. Whether they
speak too much or too little (see the distinction in Chapter 3
between 'comic heroes' and 'comic villains'), their speaking is
'out of measure'. This is one of the ways in which we can
understand the fact that comic characters are so often below
the *social* status to which they aspire: they are claiming a
discursive register which is beyond them. Comic characters
are likely to be 'low', which in itself – other things being equal
– operates to restrict implication with them. But their lowness
is a matter not simply of representing a subordinated position
in an actual social scale, but of the audience finding them (like
the Butts of social jokes) to be inept operators of the languages
they employ. In the opening of *The Alchemist*, Face and Subtle
from the very first line abuse each other in scurrilous and
obscene terms, so that we not only enjoy and disavow their
taboo-breaking but also construct each as degraded in their
association with such language. Furthermore, they are ineptly
operating the signs of social hierarchy: for while Subtle's use
of a flask of urine to ward off Face's sword is a practical and
ingenious defensive tactic, not only is it contact with a
polluting substance but it mixes a 'low' kind of brawling with
the 'high' practice of sword-fighting.

In a similar way we can understand how the presentational
style of effective comedy follows the same pattern of disjuncture between 'speaking' and effect as that represented amongst
its characters. Since what is enacted is separated on stage from

appropriate response (so that it is by definition discursively incompetent), the theatre audience, in not being implicated in the characters' feelings, can attend to the representation of all sorts of events as a speaking. As long as we understand this self-advertising disjunction to be intentional, we can laugh *with* the authorial position. This is true of any emotion, and *'Allo, 'Allo* is an outstanding demonstration that there is nothing which totally defies comic treatment. A mother crying for her dead son is, of course, moving if it is Hecuba, or Ivy Brennon mourning her Brian, while the pantomime Dame wailing because she thinks Aladdin is dead is very funny. Death is often funny: in Goldoni's *Venetian Twins* Zanetto dies at length in front of the audience, and a combination of the other characters' reactions, his 'nasty character', the plot so far, and so on, combine to make it a very comical scene. In the Ealing Brothers' 1959 film *Kind Hearts and Coronets*, seven characters are murdered; but since we have no implication with them and no other characters are distressed, we are free to laugh at this supreme example of 'improper work'.

The fate of Pyramus and Thisbe in *A Midsummer Night's Dream*'s play-within-a-play might be disallowed as an example of funny deaths, on the grounds that it is not the deaths of characters that we see, but Bottom and Flute acting badly. Yet whenever we see a performance we know that what we are watching is acting, while skilfully performed, competent scripts can produce – detail by detail – an implication which suppresses that knowledge. Inadvertent poor acting and inept writing, which Shakespeare mimics in the *Dream*, fail in what is recognisably an attempt to implicate their audience, and such plays are likely to be laughed 'at' because they have claimed a power over us that we refuse. When the ineptness is read as deliberate, we laugh 'with' what we understand to be parody.[1]

Characters are comic through a carefully structured culmination of incoherences: their behaviour is not commensurate with their (constructed) motivation; other characters' responses are not in measure with their intended effects; all their signification is inappropriate; and this incites the Audience to notice the disjuncture between the 'presentation' and 'representation' of the text. Along with this, leaving aside the balance many comedies create between 'joking' and 'implicating' moments, in what is purely joking a balance operates between our barred implication and our engagement with the action as something to 'make sense of' – much like social jokes. Comic texts use the same mechanisms as serious ones to incite the audience to find out what explains the action, what will happen next – line by line, scene by scene, and across the whole performance. But forming the answers to these puzzles, as in social jokes, involves us in violating the Symbolic Law. Comic plots are typically fast-moving and highly involved, so we are engaged to follow the action closely enough genuinely to produce transgressive doublings, excesses of signification that are, at the same time, marked – because the action is nevertheless not implicating and therefore funny.

If Shakespeare's *Antony and Cleopatra* (I, i) opened at its eighteenth line, before any implicating context had been established, it might well be understood as a comedy. At line 18 Antony and Cleopatra are together on stage when 'an Attendant' enters:

> ATTENDANT: News, my good lord, from Rome.
> ANTONY: Grates me, the sum.
> CLEOPATRA: Nay, hear them, Antony:
>   Fulvia perchance is angry; or who knows
>   If the scarce-bearded Caesar have not sent
>   His powerful mandate to you, 'Do this, or this;
>   Take in that kingdom, and enfranchise that;
>   Perform't, or else we damn thee.'
> ANTONY: How, my love?
> CLEOPATRA: Perchance? nay, and most like:
>   You must not stay here longer, your
>   dismission
>   Is come from Caesar, therefore hear it,
>   Antony.
>   Where's Fulvia's process? Caesar's I would
>   say. Both?
>   Call in the messengers. As I am Egypt's queen,
>   Thou blushest, Antony, and that blood of
>   thine
>   Is Caesar's homager: else so thy cheek pays
>   shame

> When shrill-tongued Fulvia scolds. The
>   messengers!

If Shakespeare's play really opened like this, the immediate presentation of a row (like *The Alchemist*'s) would open to a joking reading of a 'nagging' woman domineering a man, transgressing the social code of gender hierarchy – made even funnier by his being otherwise a powerful figure, a commanding soldier. 'How, my love?' is a classically comic male response – indexing confusion and ineffectual placating – to a comically powerful female tirade such as Cleopatra's. Furthermore, the language is comically self-advertising, with the Queen's parodic exaggeration of Caesar's commands and the Attendant's message and Antony's response absurdly, and so self-advertisingly, compressed (it must always require skilful acting to deliver 'Grates me, the sum' with no comic effect). Our engagement with this action would involve no implicated response to the characters as having 'innerness' – their responses to each other in this sequence do not construct this – nor to anything except the cognitive conundrum of 'what has happened to cause this?' and 'what will happen next?'.

This is not, though, the opening of the play. Its first thirteen lines frame this row within Philo's horror of Antony's 'dotage' to a 'strumpet', so that whether the audience agrees with Philo or finds the passion (which is then shown in the remaining four lines before the Attendant arrives) self-justifying, they have been invited to relate the play's action to an implicating reality. At this point, however, the audience's implication is probably ideological rather than affective; a value system has been mobilised, so that instead of laughing at the characters' ineptness it will be read as having effect in its world and judged morally, in a way which parallels the judgements we operate in reality. All comic behaviour is 'ir-ratio-nal', but irrational behaviour is disturbing rather than funny when, like Antony's and Cleopatra's, it is constructed as indexing a psychological reality and/or some kind of value system, which it disrupts. In that case its 'badness' is threatening rather than inept, and the characters are constructed as distressingly psychologically disturbed: they have 'gone out of' the 'minds' we have constructed in relation to them.

Behaviour which is 'mad' and behaviour which is funny are definitionally alike. Objects of laughter cannot control them-selves or the world effectively; they do not make proper sense in or of the world. This is also the definition of madness, whatever particular behaviour a culture takes to manifest such inability. Not only is comic behaviour quite often produced in plots through some temporary mental aberration – such as drunkenness or 'a blow on the head' – but all broad comic behaviour would read as madness if it were read with serious implication. On the contrary, what texts present as disturbing madness will inevitably be funny if it is not accepted implicatingly.

In our present Western culture, although drunkenness is still often treated as funny, madness – whether it is mental illness or handicap – is treated as sympathetic and also as alarming; it thus generally evokes both positive and negative affective implication. Therefore, while drunkenness remains what it has always been, the very frequent 'plot excuse' for comic behaviour, madness – indexed as such – is now unlikely to be so. This has not always, of course, been the case. Real mad people have been denied implication and, consequently, found funny, as when Bedlam was a place for outings. To define someone as 'mad' then functioned, in actuality or in texts, to bar their 'realisation', in the way that comic texts operate to construct their characters. As late as 1858 Dickens could produce 'Mr F.'s aunt', a demented old lady, as a character who causes laughable embarrassment to others in *Little Dorrit*.

When madness is represented in texts from other periods, it is not always a simple matter to determine whether or not this was originally comic action. On such sites, then, we can see very clearly how the presence or absence of an audience's implication determines whether they find something funny.[2]

In Middleton's *The Changeling* we find a 'masque' of madmen which is clearly intended to be funny inasmuch as satirical comments are given to the characters: through these the authorial position communicates directly with the audi-ence, over the heads of the characters, who are thus not constructed implicatingly. It is much less clear how the 'mad masque' in Webster's *Duchess of Malfi* was intended to be received, and Ferdinand's madness in that play's last Act is at once difficult to perform seriously and disruptive (for modern audiences) if it is allowed to be funny. At least, it is disruptive if the first four Acts have been played to elicit affective implication. Arguably, that is to impose upon Webster's text something to which it is not open; whereas Shakespeare supplies obvious examples of Renaissance madmen who are clearly contextually prevented from being comic in Prince Hamlet and King Lear.

Affective implication with Lear is assured through the scripted response of other characters. For example, the scene in which the King arraigns his ungrateful daughters, in the person of 'a joint stool', before a 'judge' who is the madman Poor Tom, could be extremely funny – and a very similar scene in Aristophanes' *The Wasps*, where another mad old man, who is obsessed with serving as a juror, is set up by his son into 'trying' a dog, while calling various household objects as witnesses, is wholly comic – but Shakespeare creates pity for the man, and perhaps terror that a king should be mad, through the interpolations of Poor Tom, who is really the heroic Edgar in disguise: 'My tears begin to take his part so much, / They'll mar my counterfeiting', and so on.

Hamlet presents more of a problem, since other characters say that the Prince is mad, but – with the possible exception of Ophelia – they do not 'pity' him. However, we are given a lot of space in which to create an empathetic innerness for Hamlet (especially the soliloquies) and consequently, if he is taken as really deranged, we will find his joking lines, such as those about Polonius's corpse, grotesque and pathetic rather than funny. If Hamlet's madness is performed as a cunning ploy we may find his joking darkly funny, as a triumphing over his enemies.

Because the implication that what modern audiences give to texts is much more likely to be affective than consciously ideological, the interpolation of what could be comic madness into otherwise serious texts is dislocating for us. If we have invested imaginative energy in creating a character's inner-ness, their strong suffering will feel painful to us and their considerable mental derangement will be alarming, 'as if' it happened to us. 'Bad' characters can be psychologically empathetic in this way – Macbeth's soliloquies invite such an implicated construction, even though we see him command terrible things, like the murder of a child. Thus while we judge his actions to be evil, a modern audience is also likely to understand both Macbeth and his wife as progressively deranged. However, the operation of such subjective, affective implication can be contrasted with a more objective construction of textual characters, in which a character may be categorised as 'good' or 'bad' without our empathetic involvement. In that case, it is much less disruptive to move from a 'serious' implication, in which the bad character is truly threatening, to a joking intention in which s/he loses power – for example, by becoming mad – and so becomes a comic object. Ideological implication is not disrupted by 'bad' characters being comically punished, as long as we have not made any imaginative identification with them. In fact, that is a slow-motion version of the basic 'object of laughter' structure.

It is still possible for pantomime villains to operate in this way – to start out as genuinely frightening and yet be overcome in broadly slapstick sequences. The devils in the medieval Mystery Cycles seem to have operated like this and so, I suspect, did Ferdinand and his brother Cardinal for their original audiences. Strong and often unarticulated aesthetic biases, however, are still in operation (see Chapter 8) whereby what is 'serious = important' must be 'serious = non-joking', and what is 'serious = non-joking' is taken to be affectively implicating. I suspect that this leads past texts to be read in distorted ways, including the assumption that importantly 'bad' characters cannot be comic, so that we find 'difficulty' or 'weakness' in plays like Webster's, and in Marlowe's *Dr Faustus* (as well as insisting that Shakespeare's great comedies are 'more than' funny); whereas these texts may demonstrate that other cultures have operated different conventions regarding the possible effects of barring affective implication.

It is perfectly possible, of course, for texts to move in and out of affective implication, but once it is invoked there is a delicate balance to be maintained concerning how much comic misery can befall which characters. Texts which are, in both senses of the word, 'popular' have always offered 'a laugh, a tear' – Dickens's novels and current soap operas are obvious examples – but there is in general a hierarchy of 'comic' and 'serious' characters (the Duckworths' rows are funny, the Barlows' are moving); and both Dickens and *Coronation Street* tend to keep broadly comic and extremely affecting characters apart in separate chapters or scenes. Slight disturbance can amusingly befall serious characters, though they can never totally lose their self-command without becoming upsetting rather than funny. Conversely, habitually comic characters can be 'moving', where this is carefully set up: Hilda Ogden crying over the small parcel carried home from from her husband's deathbed has become one of the legendary moments of *Coronation Street*.

Interpolating 'serious' – i.e. affectively implicating – moments into comic texts is widely taken as a mark of their high quality. In Chapter 6 I shall discuss the overall effects of such a mixture of discursive intention; here I want only to note again that manoeuvring an audience in this way is always the result of detailed mechanisms within the texts whereby the timing, degree and site of the changed reception are controlled (to repeat the most obvious examples of predisposed sites, 'true love' is very likely to be accepted as an implicating experience even in a broadly comic character, and irritation is generally available as an amusing, but not disruptive, experience for predominantly serious characters).

There is a textual effect which involves not so much a movement between 'serious' and 'joking' intention as a constant ambiguity. Because assuming the primary intention to joke or not is a very basic move in making sense of any utterance, this is a deeply disruptive textual strategy. If a character, or a value, is constructed as implicating, it is offered as a site of 'proper' language, of language which has reference beyond itself; when a character or value is the object of joking, 'proper' language is produced in contradistinction to their 'negatively quoted' utterance – so Teller and Audience, marking error, construct the signifying system as arbitrary but still as mastered. When a text is radically ambiguous, there is no site of 'proper' language and no mastery. The effect is to deny the possibility of 'proper' language: to declare us all mad. In the later twentieth century several texts have been taken to operate in this way: Pinter and Beckett are obvious examples. Literary criticism has not only celebrated what J. L. Styan called the 'dark comedy' of these modern texts, but pointed to its presence in past texts. 'Tragicomedy' has often been declared the dominant dramatic form of the twentieth century, and performances of past texts, following the critics' line, were staged to emphasise that aspect (see Styan; Corrigan, 1981, pp. 222–7; Howarth, pp. 165–86; and consider, for example the 1979 Royal Shakespeare Company production of *King Lear* in which Antony Sher played the Fool, which emphasised similarities between scenes in the play and vaudeville routines and, in the programme, explicitly linked Shakespeare's text with *Waiting for Godot*).

Such a disruption of language – which is like joking in denying any secure reference to something real outside language, yet unlike joking in not offering a distinct position from which to construct alternative, *discursively* effective language – is typical of 'Modernism'. Antony Easthope, making specific reference to T. S. Eliot, Beckett and Pinter, lists amongst that movement's characteristics 'open[ing] the text to a polysemic interplay in which no syntagmatic chain achieves automatic privilege' (1989, p. 170). The production – and, more so, the critical celebration – of such a textual strategy is rather problematic, because the total negativity they suggest is at odds with the position of cultural authority the texts actually construct. When we find them in any way pleasurable or empowering, we must construct a position from which it 'makes sense' to assert that there is 'no sense'. It is a little suspicious that such a strategy can still be taken as peculiar proof of a text's quality.

Alan Ayckbourn's reputation significantly shifted from that of mere farceur to serious dramatist following the 1985 production of his *Woman in Mind*. Once he had written a play with a definitely unhappy ending, the skill and perception in his earlier work received much more critical notice. In this play a woman whose family comically disregards her frustration progresses to total mental breakdown. When she has her first collapse, at the beginning of the play, Susan – and the audience – hear the other characters speaking a nonsensically distorted language. In this first scene, where we have no reason to be implicated with Susan or with the clownishly inept doctor, this creates a comic 'mutual misunderstanding' sequence. Throughout the rest of the play we come to see the selfish family through Susan's eyes, via her wry comments when she is sane and the contrasting, adoring family presented in her hallucinations. Thus we come to empathise with Susan, constructing psychological depth in the character and, indeed, accepting her as the play's only 'proper' speaker. In the last scene, in a considerable technical *tour de force*, Susan loses all contact with reality and herself produces the nonsensically distorted language: 'Hair shone? Hair hall shone? Tone show, fleas' (i.e. 'Where've you gone? Where've you all gone? Don't go, please'). What is – in the most basic sense – 'improper' speech has been directly reversed from the laughable, joking presentation of the opening scene to the disturbing, implicating madness of the ending, because we are no longer engaged across, but directly through it.

The creation or barring of implication can be observed here as a specific operation of the presentational language of drama, producing a complexly effective shift from joking to serious textual address (the opposite of *The Duchess of Malfi*). Explicitly 'mad' characters exhibit the location of 'proper' language that a text elects (or its absence), but they are an anomaly in comedy. Paradigmatically, to the extent that a text is joking, the author position and the Audience share and affirm their own discursive propriety across characters who have enough discursive ability to make it worthwhile to construct them as objects of laughter whose ineptness distinguishes 'them' from 'us'.

Notes

1. I am not suggesting that the *only* way in which a play can be 'serious' is through transparently naturalistic presentation; but at this point I am comparing plays which are effective in that way with plays which aim at but fail to achieve the effect, and noting the comic presentation which *advertises* the gap.
2. Although the direction and acting of a script can make a lot of difference to the audience's response, it remains sensible to ask

whether a script (a) has lines and implied actions that make sense *only* as serving to evoke implication; and (b) how far it remains otherwise coherent when 'business' or delivery is introduced that excites – or bars – affective/ideological engagement.

5

Exchange as the Language of Comedy

If joking always involves an unusual attention to language, we can see comedies as joking texts which, by barring the audience's implication, produce their action in its aspect as language. In this chapter I shall suggest that the *behavioural* language comedy thus treats is 'the discourse of exchange'.

For this argument to be clear, the terms 'language' and 'discourse' (i.e. language-in-use) must be taken in their fullest sense. Ideally we need another term to encompass all our 'making sense' activity, which involves much more than words, since these two are persistently associated with *verbal* signification; but the only candidate, 'signifying structures', abstracts the structures from their active use in a way that can be highly misleading, so I shall go on speaking of joking's negotiations of 'discursive competence' and ask readers to remember the definition of 'language-as-such' that I proposed in Chapter 1: the operation of the rule of 'same and different' which allows elements to 're-present' each other, when they are restricted 'ratio-nally' to one signifier and one signified in one semantic space. In that chapter I pointed to Lacan's finding, in Lévi-Strauss's treatment of 'exchange as a form of communication', the generation of a fundamental 'meaning' produced by obeying this Law, which is prior to any message, whereby the subject self is confirmed when an utterance is received by a significant Other as Symbolically 'proper' language. I have suggested that joking is a strong operation of this fundamental meaning, because Teller and Audience collusively breach the Symbolic Law but, in marking their transgression, affirm their ultimate compliance with it; while the objects of their laughter are constructed as breaching but not marking the rule, and so as discursively incompetent, degraded, others.

Thus the targets of joking become 'objects' in *our* language because they are (constructed as) unable to make their effect in the world; sometimes we deny them discursive power because they are 'de-graded' (by contamination, for example); sometimes it is their 'irratio-nality' – which can be any kind of inappropriate discourse – that in itself degrades them from 'potent' to 'impotent'. When targets make discursive errors, that language is itself usually funny, but we can just laugh 'at' a target for being 'stupid' (they alone, not what they say, are the site of the Audience's linguistic manipulation). That will not happen in punch-line jokes, where there is only time to establish any speaker as the set-up for an isolated 'excess signification', but in the extended world of comic texts we are dealing with 'funny characters' who, being incompetent, must be either 'knaves' or 'fools': too dishonest or too stupid to discourse properly. In consequence we are dealing with constructed *intentions* as qualifying the discursive propriety of our objects. What amounts to the same thing is that in comic works we are engaged with characters' actions at some length, with an enacted plot and so with 'signification' that is by definition concerned with *doing* rather than only *saying* (although the action can, of course, be described in words and usually involves their use). To pursue this: the particular but fundamental behavioural 'language' with which comedy texts can be seen to deal is that of 'exchange', in which the discursive incompetence of the objects is essentially established by the false relation between the elements they exchange and the 'self' that extorts recognition.

In the individual jokes/gags of comic drama, its enacted behaviour may appear as linguistically 'proper' or 'improper' because it becomes involved with separable Symbolic hierarchies and their associated taboos – touching dirty things, for example, or revealing your knickers in inappropriate circumstances. Its overall plots, however, are particularly involved with behavioural language that is constituted by actions which in themselves *form*, rather than contingently *acquire*, significance. This can be approached through Lévi-Strauss's definition of a society as 'individuals and groups which communicate with one another' and the additional specification that 'in any society, communication operates on three levels: communication of women, communication of goods and services, communication of messages' (1972, p. 296). In this theorisation all activities of material exchange, being understood as 'communication', appear as 'a kind of language', while verbal language, in parallel, appears as (amongst other things) a kind of exchange when its structures are 'communicated', i.e. used in discourse. 'Exchange' can thus be examined as a kind of behaviour which, besides its obvious practical effects, also produces 'meaning' – the participants' identity as subjective agents – and is therefore a kind of language.

Although it is not clear that Lévi-Strauss consistently takes 'communication' to imply what I have assumed of 'discourse' – that it constitutes individuals' subjectivity by definition in its passage between them – such an interpretation does yield a coherent reading of his work in this area – further validated when we notice how particularly this discussion of 'exchange as communication' influenced Lacan's formulations of 'language' in the 'Rome Discourse'.[1] How far Lévi-Strauss's theory stands as a solution to the anthropological conundrum of kinship structures, in which context it was originally proposed, I do not know. However, this formulation functions very usefully as a bridge to understanding comedy *plot* as representing a form of 'mis-usable' language. Even before their implications are fully unpacked, we can observe how suggestively Lévi-Strauss's categories of exchange coincide with the most persistent comic plots.

The 'exchange of women', otherwise known as 'the Romance plot', has often been identified as 'the most usual basis of comedy' (Frye, 1957, p. 163): it appears in all comic traditions, from Greek New Comedy to tomorrow's television situation comedy. The other most characteristic comic subject, the matter of 'satirical' as opposed to 'romantic' comedy, involves the inept 'exchange of goods and services': the tricky comic hero tries to gain more than he gives; the blocking villain tries to gain while giving nothing. Lévi-Strauss's third category, 'exchange of messages', can be taken to cover the verbal and conceptual joking that occurs within most comedy, and as we consider the sense in which verbal language in itself involves an 'exchange' of the power of discursive identity, the 'inept exchange' constituted by bragging and snobbery – which feature so often in comedy – becomes clearer.

Lévi-Strauss first and most fully described 'exchange' as 'a form of communication' in relation to 'the exchange of women'; identifying this as:

> a kind of language, a set of processes permitting the establishment, between individuals and groups, of a certain kind of communication. That the mediating factor, in this case, should be the *women of the group*, who are circulated between clans, lineages, or families, in place of the *words of the group*, which are circulated between individuals, does not at all change the fact that the essential aspect of the phenomenon is identical in both cases. (1972, p. 61; original emphasis)

I want to bracket here the obvious contradictions involved in only male persons 'exchanging' only females. At this point, to understand exactly what Lévi-Strauss means by calling exchange a kind of language, we must note that he draws a parallel between 'women' as *people* and 'words': this argument would not be altered if males were exchanged. Lévi-Strauss proposes that women are exchanged between *groups* 'as' words are exchanged between *individuals*.

What I think is implicit but not spelled out in Lévi-Strauss's formulation is that in relation to exchange, 'words' are not being considered as semantically complex signs. In the totality of their signifying function, words involve that fixed double structure of signifier and signified through which they designate; but their operation of 'wording the world' is additional to, or abstractable from, the operation in which *all* discourse functions proleptically to constitute the recognised identity of sender and receiver.

When material exchange is considered as a discourse (in separation from its direct material rearrangements – eggs for milk, etc.) its elements do acquire a binary nature. In use, whilst having objective standing – i.e. they recognisably exist to *be* exchanged (they are things understood to have exchange values) – they also 'mean' the speakers' identity. However, the binary nature of 'exchange elements', whether they are goods, people or words, occurs only in their actual use: it can only be performed, while the binary nature of complex 'signs' is intrinsic – their designation can and must (up to a point) be permanently codified.

Thus what Lévi-Strauss is proposing is that *as elements of exchange* 'women' establish the distinct identities of the exchanging groups. The patterns of kin relationships which determine whom a woman should marry are constituted *through* the activity of exchange, so that instead of seeing pre-existing groups who have certain formulae of marital exchange, we can turn the process on its head and see the exchanging activity as producing the identifiable groups which form the 'positions' that are the sites of the kinship pattern. At the same time women also obviously exist as objective entities, individual people. In parallel, words are 'objective entities' in existing as permanent signs within the group's language, separable from the individuals who use them, but whose identity as subjective agents is established when they use words in verbal discursive exchange. What is also implicit is the typically Lévi-Straussian pattern of entities mediating between separated categories because they are constructed to involve elements of both – in exchange, both 'women' and 'words' involve the identity of an individual and the identity of the group; and also the inversional parallel, in which it is 'individual' women who mediate between groups and 'group' words that mediate between individuals.

Words will always, then, have this 'discursive exchange' function when they are in use – constituting a kind of language which is separable from their designating function (although the *sociological* 'identity value' established will be involved with their users' designating competence); and – again in parallel – any material exchange which directly involves its participants will also have some effect of *discursive* exchange. When language is considered in the context of its relationship to psychic formations and the constitution of the self, its aspect as exchange appears to be fundamental: the fundamental 'ratio-nal' rule of one Symbolic entity to one semantic space is at once possible and necessary because of its effect in producing identity when it is enacted: a recognised exchange must, by definition, obey the rule, and that *is* language. We must note, though, that the 'giving and taking' of discursive identity operates the opposite way round from economic exchange.

In material exchange the giver is the loser, for if I give you something, then I do not have it; fair exchange then depends on receiving something of equal value to what one has given.[2] Words are puzzling 'objects of exchange' in that case, because if I 'give' you words, I have not lost anything (as Leach irritably insists: p. 110). However, it is not in 'giving' words, but in their *being received* that identity is constituted – as we have already seen in locating the crucial 'joking utterance' as the Audience's silent response confirmed by the 'listening' Teller, and as Lacan describes the primary confirmation of one's agency in 'the call' being 'received' by an other. What we swop in discourse is the power of identity, and what is given away in all speaking is the *listener's* attention.

Power in discourse belongs most obviously to the speaker, but that is at the cost of seeking confirmation from the listener(s) – it is the capacity to command such recognition which constitutes the speaker's discursive power. Whenever the participants are directly involved with each other, *material* exchange has some tincture of this discursive operation, in which the identity/authority of the donor is constituted by the attention or respect it extorts from the receiver, over and above any material reciprocation. The paradoxical power of giving to extort identity confirmation can be observed in any pub when negotiations of 'Whose round?' occur: people who get away with not buying a fair share of drinks save money, but lose face; people trying to establish an insecure social identity often insist on buying more drinks than they accept.

The 'inept' speaking of exchange discourse, as opposed to mismatching signifieds and signifiers, is to offer or accept false value; and although economic cheating may be involved, in its discursive aspect the value that inept exchange falsifies is 'identity': at a very basic level, and however it is manifested, someone is seeking more power-of-agency than they deserve. To identify cheating exchange as 'improper' discourse is not simply a metaphor – it is a kind of false speech, whether it is motivated by dishonesty or stupidity, for the identity whose recognition it extorts has not really been performed.

In this way, all exchange involves the functioning of a signifying system, and when a comedy's audience experience such behaviour as *funny* (as a whole, on top of individual jokes and gags) they transgress in doubly producing its action as viable and as non-viable, while also 'marking' the characters' errors against a 'proper' operation which they themselves produce and master. If there were not the doubling of simultaneous vicarious enjoyment and disowning, there would be *only* fantasy pleasure, with discursive judgement wholly suspended; or only disapproval. Yet in attending to action as exchange we are attending to it as language, and this unusual awareness will probably produce the matter as funny where some apparently absolute value is put in the light of a conventional – i.e. linguistic – construct.

Thus we can begin to pick out the ways in which the action of comic dramas, whether it is concerned with manipulating material goods or words, involves false exchange which operates as a transgressive use of language. Comic characters, like Subtle and Face (and from Aristophanes' Socrates to Del Boy), acquire 'goods and services' without proper reciprocation; they claim women to whom they are not, within an implied norm, entitled and/or they refuse discourse altogether: for example, *not* exchanging their daughters. Comic 'theft' is often actually fraud, involving claims to undeserved *status* – the number of examples is overwhelming – and a characteristically twentieth-century twist makes the thief an unlikely or inefficient felon, undeservedly claiming criminal status – as in the Ealing Brothers' *The Lavender Hill Mob*. Even when it is not a con trick, comic theft generally involves ingenuity (like the *Lavender Hill Mob*'s stolen gold exported cast as Eiffel Tower souvenirs) or a cunning dexterity, like the cutpurse Nightingale in *Bartholomew Fair*, conceptual manipulations which parallel the con man's verbal manipulation.

Separably from but often as part of fraudulent activity, comic characters try to use authoritative verbal language whose power of identity they have not earned because they are deliberately lying about, or stupidly misunderstanding, what they say. Bragging and snobbish aspiration are thus, in the discourse of exchange, parallel to material cheating: Mrs Malaprop's crucially funny Symbolic ineptitude is mistakenly believing she commands a high status by using erudite words that are in fact erroneous; local funny moments arise through her mangled would-be-elite vocabulary, but the discourse of 'exchange', not of verbal language's dictionary, forms the site of the overall joking.

It will help to understand why particular sites of exchange may recurrently figure in comedy plots if we notice that in the same way as social jokes – when our laughter confirms that we have marked what the comic characters do as breaching both convention and the Symbolic Law – comedies dynamically affirm what constitutes 'proper' performance on those sites their plots negotiate. Since this discourse of exchange forms the constituting base of any 'society', while particular so-cieties' definitions of how and what it is 'proper' to exchange are highly contingent, comedy appears as a potent force for establishing a given society's conventions as internalised norms – as forms whose observance is entailed with full subjectivity. Laughing at comedy, we exercise the power of 'othering' its false exchangers, but we are also incited to identify ourselves through formulations of 'proper' exchange. If what is dominantly constructed as 'proper' exchange were always unproblematically fair to all parties, this would present neither cognitive nor political difficulty; but the complexity inherently present and/or ideologically entailed in much conventionally validated 'exchange' suggests first that these sites will be those especially available to the energies of joking, because they generate tensions whose relief is urgent. Secondly, comedy's tendency to address and to suture socioeconomic contradictions that might be better explored openly appears.[3] Thus a further characteristic of comedy's typical sites of exchange becomes apparent: those whose operation is unequally available or rewarding to all the members of a society.

When we look at what is most often 'exchanged' in comedy, we find elements that are intrinsically ambiguous, within discourses that have developed as especially contradictory – for example, where words also constitute some kind of economic 'work', so that their labour-value exchange is easily mistaken. Again, comedy flourishes where economic power is ideologically confused with natural status, as in negotiations of familial relationships, especially marriage; but also any work situation to the extent that the boss is accorded *social* authority. All articulated social hierarchies tend to be contradictory because birth, wealth and intelligence are all 'high' qualities which do not, in fact, always coincide, so that they are prone to confusion (servants cleverer than masters) and the cheating/mistaking of snobbery.

All material exchange, as Cowie's definition of 'the giving and receiving of different but equivalent items' (p. 51) reminds us, always requires a discursive operation which equates 'different items' – different kinds of objects, different kinds of labour; and this is why it is inherently difficult and contradictory. People do not value things only in terms of the labour it takes to produce them, or their survival value; ideological values are also involved, so opportunities for faking and mistaking abound. Again, there is an inherent potential contradiction between the power of accumulating wealth and the power of giving it away. In both cases there remains, at least notionally, a possibility of 'fair exchange', in which all parties benefit equally and discursive identity formation is not at odds with economic advantage. However, societies develop other 'exchange' situations whose contradictions are perhaps impossible to resolve, because they are ideologically produced in terms of abstract values that function to suppress the economic exchange they entail: as the vocabulary of 'duty' directly denies that any exchange of labour-value is entailed in, for example, master–servant or wife–husband relations.

It is possible to redescribe most – if not all – comedy plots in terms other than 'exchange', just as it is possible to explain most social jokes in many different, yet accurate ways, because their elements are always multiply referential and active. However, 'exchange' can be seen as the unifying linguistic mode that comic texts bring to Audiences' attention, and this formulation can be made more precise. The sites of most exchange in complex societies, though, are more involved than the direct barter of object for object. The mediating stages of labour and (often) cash bring most economic exchange into the category 'work'. A structure of comic characters can be identified in which their particular 'inept speaking' can be compared to Freud's categorisation of personality type described in terms of 'inept workers'.

In practice 'work' is almost always, like language, an activity involving exchange with others. Indeed, language *is* a kind of work, for its effects are produced with effort, at cost.[4] Further, the exchange of labour, like that of language, involves a social gamble – something must be 'given' *before* its equivalent can be received – but there is no alternative to this gamble, for economically – as psychically – exchanging is necessary to survival. Thus Lévi-Strauss's three categories of exchange are not wholly distinct; rather, the exchange of 'value' appears as a basic pattern of human activity, taking three forms that are at once parallel and continually inter-involved.[5] The exchange of women is not separate from the other two, for of course it will entail speaking words 'as' the constituted group identity and, very often, material exchange; while it fundamentally exhibits the structure of giving first in order to get later, producing the constantly operating 'Great Debt' to which all must be subject if language-as-such is to be possible. 'Work' – given all the modulations to which the term is open,[6] all the ideological contradictions its constructions accrue, and its intrinsic inter-involvement of material and discursive exchange – can be seen as a key concept in analysing the particular sites comedy texts represent.

Thus work is often culturally imaged as a solitary and self-satisfying effort – someone labouring to produce something for their own consumption in a way that is very similar to the picture of language as an autonomous production. In this way an idea(l) of work as something we do by ourselves and for ourselves – 'satisfying' labour – parallels the construction of language as a speaking to oneself which may incidentally, secondarily, be directed as communication to others.[7] At its extremes, we know that this is madness: the private language of Dante's giant, the self-produced world of Ayckbourn's Susan in her happier phase. The phantasy of language at our command is one of comedy's most obvious Imaginary pleasures, as we identify with comic 'heroes' who – for a space

– evade the paradox that at neither material nor linguistic levels can we 'produce ourselves' independently of others' exchanging reception.

Freud's three 'arrested' and fourth, 'mature' personalities are defined in terms of their illegitimately *taking* what they need from others or producing it for themselves. Erich Fromm, a Marxist psychoanalyst, explicitly connected this with modes of economic production, and his summaries of the four types of 'worker' offer a highly suggestive schema defining the pattern of characteristics which are found in comedy characters. Furthermore, it can be extended to exhibit the identification of 'work' and 'language' so that this schema aligns with my argument that joking always negotiates the 'cost' of exchanging language, and that comedy deals especially with the language of material exchange.

Freud's four categories are set out most clearly in 'Character and anal eroticism' (1908b); Fromm discusses these in *Greatness and Limitations of Freud's Thought* (1982). The first of the stages which, in this formulation, all must pass but some never leave, is the 'oral receptive' defined by Fromm as the person 'who expects to be fed, materially, emotionally and intellectually. He [*sic*] is the person with the "open mouth", basically passive and dependent, who expects that what he needs will be given to him' (p. 55). Greek 'New Comedy' (i.e. later than Aristophanes) offers a precise parallel to this infantile aberration in the stock figure of 'the Parasite', whose action in the plays is almost wholly confined to wangling dinner invitations – quite literally managing to be fed without working. Since the wangling involves flattery and trickery, he opens towards that most recognisable of comic characters, the 'trickster', who lives by fooling others through false deals and clever speech. A list of such characters is harder to stop than to start: they range through the Greek and Roman 'tricky slaves', Harlequino, Falstaff, Del Boy (of *Only Fools and Horses* – the full implied title, 'Only Fools and Horses Work', expresses the pattern precisely), Arthur Daley and, of course, Subtle and Face, Volpone, Molière's confidence tricksters . . . and so on.

In both Freudian and comedy structures, this category runs over into the next, the 'oral sadistic' who also 'believes that everything he needs comes from outside and not through his own work. But unlike the oral-receptive character he does not expect anyone to give him what he wants voluntarily, but tries to take what he needs from others by force' (Fromm, p. 55). As we have seen, comic characters tend to cheat rather than thieve, so that their exchange may be deceptive rather than totally absent. Typically, they try to cheat one another, each believing that they are taking more than they give. One effect of this is that since no 'good exchanger' is produced in the play world, the theatre audience are not incited to an implicating sympathy with what would be an innocent victim. The trickery remains available to construction as inept discourse, and the audience enjoy their identificatory pleasure with the successful embezzler while they construct for themselves the 'proper discourse' against which this is marked as mistaken.

Comic attempts to take something by force are more often an illegitimate claim to authority than a literal robbery with violence: efficient violence will be funny only when its victim is a degraded, partly powerful Butt (as when, for example, Chaplin's 'Little Tramp' turns the tables on a bully, or Molière's Scapin contrives to beat his master Géronte in *Les Fourberies de Scapin*, Act III, Scene ii). In discursive if not moral terms the authority extorted by efficient violence is perfectly legitimate, while comic characters pretend to respect that which they do not really merit: they may try to use physical force – as in the memorable scene where Woody Allen's armed bank raid fails because the clerk misreads his threatening note – but words are the more usual weapon, sliding from outright lying (like Subtle and Face), down through scales of self-awareness, to stupidity (e.g. Mrs Malaprop). The energy of response evoked by our both identifying with and disowning comic false speakers (which I discussed in Chapter 3) is often enhanced by the effect that they are carried away by their own fabrication: as they are victims of their own energy, their speech thus remains false, without being morally culpable. Falstaff (for example in the story of the proliferating buckram men) or the Hancock character's belief in his own 'calighber', are examples; as, arguably, is Subtle.

All comic authority figures, inasmuch as they are degraded and shown to be inept (as Chapter 3 discussed), are false exchangers in this way, from Malvolio to Captain Mainwaring. Any character aspiring to power or admiration they do not properly earn is cheating in the exchange of attention. They are often snobs, and snobbery establishes itself as a comic characteristic (and a word) at the beginning of the seventeenth century, when considerable social mobility became a real possibility, and flourishes until it is difficult to think of many comic characters in the twentieth century who do not have some snobbery. In societies which allowed very little social mobility, the most evident way for a male to increase his social standing was through warfare; the 'braggart soldier' is (fairly) deliberately lying in his claims to discursive authority on the basis of heroic battle action. He runs through New Comedy and commedia dell'arte's Spanish Captains; he begins – as, for example, Shakespeare's Pistol and Jonson's Bobbadil – to meet snobs in his world in the seventeenth century, and is gradually almost entirely replaced in the comic pattern by them, as falsifiable social authority becomes more variously available.

Literary criticism has predominantly focused on the individual, psychological characteristics of comic 'villains', or on their function of 'blocking' festivity or fecundity; but this can hardly occur without involving sociological transgression, as 'moral correction' theories of the genre imply. Although some traditional criticism aligns the blocking character *with* 'society' – and so against the hero's individuality (see Chapter 8) – the Audience must construct it as normatively incorrect, almost by definition. Ambiguity may occur: the society represented in a text may bear no resemblance to its Audience's actuality; while in cases where actual institutional prescriptions fail to match prevalent behavioural norms, precisely the kind of discursive contradiction arises which comedy typically explores, but concentrating on individual psychology or its inversion as mythic pattern may divert attention from the unambiguous social transgressions pre-twentieth-century Audiences would have recognised in comic characters.

Malvolio is not just a misery opposed to Belch's roistering, he is a hierarchically ambiguous top servant trying to invert the delicate balance of status between himself and the hierarchically marginal bottom aristocrat; he further believes that he can totally transform his status through the tendentious route of marrying a superior woman – the same social anomaly tragically presented in *The Duchess of Malfi* (where Antonio's wife calls him by the Twelfth Night title 'Lord of Misrule': Act III Scene ii). Mainwaring, in the peculiar conditions of wartime, is a petty-bourgeois recapturing the old opportunity for military prowess to advance social standing, a *miles gloriosus* whose mild pretensions are gently, persistently undercut by Sergeant Wilson's genuine upper-class diffidence. These characters are claiming undeserved status and thus falsifying their exchangeable identity.

Whatever psychological or other pattern can be identified, a comic character is always involved not only with a social but specifically with a discursive transgression. Social and psychic identity formations are inseparable, as Freud's definition of psychological types in terms of 'work' actually implies, but the discursive aspect of their behaviour must be foregrounded in comic characters, not least because otherwise they would be implicating and unfunny. The particular behaviour constructed as discursively incompetent may alter with changing social arrangements, producing contradictions in the process; comedy generally reflects current as well as recurrent areas of ambiguity, even if it uses historical settings.

An example is twentieth-century comedy's concentration on family life, on relationships after rather than negotiations towards marriage. Husbands and wives who break the rules of faithfulness and gender hierarchy have been the stuff of farce (defined below) from Plautus through Heywood's *Jan Jan and Sir Johan the Priest* to Feydeau; but television produced situation comedy whose comically imbalanced situation is 'normal' marriage, and stage plays such as Ayckbourn's followed suite. Such shows continue to be popular, while permutations of 'unusual' (rather than farcically disrupted) families abound: two female parents, two male parents, wife as breadwinner, and so on. It is generally acknowledged that such settings, often deliberately, reflect contemporary conditions: I am emphasising that they also manifest basic patterns of individuals (mis)-negotiating discursive exchange; while past texts equally display both universal structures of erroneous exchange and their contemporary socially problematic sites.

Identifying the re-presentation of 'exchange as discourse' in all comedy helps to avoid misleading separations of the universal and the socially local, of public and private, personal and political – distinctions traditional literary criticism, especially in relation to comedy, tends to foster.

Where social hierarchies are considerably immobile, we are likely to meet the character who refuses all exchange more often than the 'false' climbers taking advantage of potential social mobility. These represent Freud's final category of arrested personality, the 'anal-sadistic' who, in Fromm's description, 'does not feel that anything new is ever created; the only way to have something is to save what they have' (p. 55). This, of course, is essentially the comic miser; but what is hoarded need not only be money. It might, for example, be a daughter (or female 'ward', as in Menander's *Duskolos*, the earliest 'social' comedy we have). The 'elderly master' charac- ters of commedia dell'arte epitomise the traditional range of comedy's anal misers: old (i.e. opposed to change), rich, miserable and greedy, while the servant characters display the basic 'oral' manifestations: youthful whatever their years, poor, cheerful and greedy.

Besides parsimony, Freud associated 'anality' with excessive orderliness and stubbornness, inept characteristics that oppose the messy errors of socially compliant orals, as in most of commedia's master/servant confrontations, as Malvolio opposes Sir Toby and, on a less 'heroic' scale, as Margot opposes the neighbours who disrupt suburban decorum with their 'Good' life. At their extremes the 'orals' and the 'anals' form up on two sides of inept exchange, one seen to take too much and offer too little, or nothing, or something false in return; the other refusing to join in exchange at all, wanting only to take (or keep) and not to give anything. But comedy does not, of course, always work at extremes, and since the two sides form the single 'coin' of inept exchange, few *major* comic characters are confined to a single aspect of it.

Memorable comic characters are often complexly located across a grid of hoarding, and seeking falsely to exchange, women/goods/status – in particular, the excessively mean or conventional often turn out, delightfully, to be hypocrites out for improper gains. (This returns us again to Chapter 3's 'falsely held power'.) The 'failure of self-knowledge' identified in comic characters as long ago as Plato's *Philebus* may be involved here, but modifying their threat rather than prompting condemnation: just as we noted that characters are more 'forgivable' – and so less genuinely threatening – when their excess language production fools themselves, so a Mainwaring or a Margot remains sympathetic because their snobbish aspirations are largely unaware. However, an Alceste or a Zeal-of-the-Land Busy (in *Bartholomew Fair*) knows perfectly well what they are about. They are commensurately fiercely punished, and the difficulty of staging Malvolio's baiting to a modern audience may be related to our sympathy for his lack of self-insight outweighing, for us, the enormity of his pretension to Olivia's hand. Again, it is at a crossroad of ambiguity or contradiction in 'discourses of exchange' that all comic characters can most consistently be located.

Contradictions also arise when characters are caught in more than one exchange discourse, making contradictory demands. Contradictory demands typically encompass the downfall of mythic and tragic heroes (Oedipus, Wotan, Oisin, Arthur, Hamlet . . .) so that, again, it is not the plot pattern but its mode of representation which distinguishes comedy. Where the mythic hero meets conflicting absolute obligations, the comic character is seen caught in contingent – albeit urgent – paradoxes whose socially coded demands cannot all be successfully met. A common twentieth-century version pits personal relationships against those of work, either on a commercial site (shops, factories, 'On the Buses') or in the home (a wife's work status is higher than her husband's, etc.).

Freud's fourth personality type, that of achieved maturity, is sexually 'genital' and as Fromm notes, 'very vague' (p. 56). Freud has defined character in terms of solutions to the problem of 'getting what we need from outside' (Fromm, p. 57), and the fourth, successful, type can be understood as 'producing' rather than 'being given, robbing [or] hoarding' (p. 57). Fromm's complaint is that Freud implicitly assumes that production involves a bourgeois 'effort of organising and using the work of others' (p. 56); but since using the work of others is part of what is immature in the first three, arrested, stages I would suggest a different understanding of this ideal personality as primarily producing himself what he consumes.[8] In unpacking what it effaces we may approach the reasons for Freud's construction of human character in terms of 'work'; and beyond that the reason why his scheme of personalities should fit so neatly into characteristic comedy structures – which will suggest a different construction of his 'mature' personality.

Defining the good worker as producing what 'he' consumes evokes an isolated self-sufficiency that can hardly exist outside fantasy – the most extreme subsistence farmer is unlikely to survive, and certainly cannot produce another generation, without a wife/husband division of labour. Even in technologically simple cultures, some people work at one thing, others at another, and to survive they must *exchange* their labour and its product. The nineteenth century separated the idea of labour from the production and exchange of labour-value, and invested such 'honest toil' with ideological value, as Carlyle in 1843 spoke of 'the nobleness, even sacredness, in work' in *Past and Present*. That valorisation in itself is probably one reason why Freud thought of 'bad and good work' as a figure of immature/mature sexuality; moreover, 'work's' suppression of the individual's physical dependence on economic exchange directly parallels the suppression of mental identity's dependence on discursive exchange, which is entailed in the atomic, self-sustaining bourgeois 'self' who produces language autonomously. Freud's writings significantly undermine that construction of self, but without quite directly articulating the constitution of identity in discourse. Given that perspective, it is possible to respeak 'the mature personality' as 'the good exchanger' (as its genital sexuality might reasonably imply): and that is the position into which the comedy audience construct themselves.

Like all joking, comedy reconciles conflicting models of identity construction: on top of pleasures offered by other aberrant discursive modes, it *confirms* (rather than suppressing or opposing) our dependence on Symbolic observance and the interpersonality which that implies; but by creating us as masters of discourse, it removes the subservience from our subjection.

Notes

1. This construction of language is central to Lacan's post–1953 thought, and the psychoanalyst's formulation is explicitly indebted to Lévi-Strauss's investigation of kinship and the incest 'taboo'. Yet, as I have indicated, this construction is not fully developed in the anthropological work. Lévi-Strauss operates a distinction between 'language-as-such' and 'verbal language' which is not articulated. His failure to distinguish clearly between 'language-as-such' and 'verbal language' makes his theorisation of the 'exchange of women as a kind of language' confusing. One result has been feminist critics' dealing with it as the belief that women function identically with signs, i.e. that they form signifiers, and a consequent search for their signified – see, for example, Cowie. As I discuss in Chapter 7, this has also been conflated with the differential access of males and females to language that psycho-analytic theories have claimed.

2. Therefore there has to be a 'third point' which both parties agree as establishing the propriety of each stage in any exchange: in buying something, the monetary conventions to which Saussure refers in his initial identification of language as a structure of 'values'; in pre-technological societies' 'exchange of women', the 'Great Debt' that Lévi-Strauss stipulates as generating each kinswoman's 'giving away'; in the Symbolic, fundamentally, the 'Law' that Lacan describes as parallel to this (1977a, p. 67). Most exchanges, of course, also involve agreed codes of usage such as dictionary definitions, or the classification of objects as clean/dirty, etc. – the particular usages negotiated in particular jokes.

3. The conventional formulations of 'proper' exchange we construct as laughing Audiences may in fact be damagingly restrictive to us, as well as to other people. For example, as a character Mrs Malaprop combines several constructions: amongst these, she is a stupidly inept power-seeker and also an elderly woman. In a society where women as a whole – and especially elderly women – are abjected, a connection between her gender and her 'discursive incompetence' is more likely to be constructed than if the character were male – that is to say, in actuality women are often seen to 'fail' as women, where men 'fail' as (ungendered) individuals, and comic characters will support such constructions. Again, Mrs Malaprop is stupidly inept in believing that her vocabulary earns high status when she really uses it mistakenly; in relation to other characters to whom the play allows legitimate authority, this constructs the competent use of complex vocabulary as 'proper'.

That confirmation of a particular verbal mode as inherently 'legitimate' may not be particularly problematic, but the operation whereby the particular usage is conjoined to symbolic efficacy without examination can be more questionable – as in *The Taming of the Shrew* when Bianca's compliance articulates the female 'norm' of willing participation in the exchange of women, from which Kate 'comically' departs.

4. That producing language always involves unwelcome effort may be seen in the way most people will answer a question without speaking where this can be done courteously and simply – for example, most people's response to the question 'What are you reading?' is to *show* the book's cover. Language production really is a kind of 'work', an effortful production, so that apparently producing it without any effort, as when we talk 'nonsense', is an intrinsically pleasurable psychic economy (as Freud [1905] notes). It is 'fun' for adults as well as children to babble meaningless syllables, and it is of course 'funny', often hysterically so, when we mark the radical transgression involved in this false linguistic production.

5. In dealing with the three types of exchange which 'constitute a society', Lévi-Strauss describes the 'exchange of commodities' as a mediating middle ground between that of 'women' (as the simplest form of language) and that of 'messages' (as the most complex), because commodity exchanges also involve verbal interactions (1972, p. 297). He also – confusingly – elaborates the identification of women as elements of language by referring to them as 'values' – that is, apparently, 'something important' – and adding: 'poets know . . . that words were once also values'. If this leads us to align non-verbal elements with 'language' because, in reverse, words may be regarded in a poetical-magical-primitive way as 'things', it is deeply misleading; it is by dismissing any reification of 'words' that Saussure focuses attention upon the *structural* 'essence' of language. That is the point of his defining words and *any element in any linguistic structure* as a 'value' in the mathematical sense of the term.

However, Lévi-Strauss's use of the term 'value' suggests, if it does not fully examine, an important relationship between material exchange and language. Marx distinguished between the effort needed to produce goods and their worth in commodity transactions in terms of their 'labour-value' and their 'exchange value'. This reminds us (amongst other things) that human efforts for survival become part of cultural consciousness at the point where they are exchanged and are thus necessarily conceptually encoded. We might speculate about the actual temporal priority, in some lost prehistory, of exchanging women and exchanging goods as our ancestors' first development of 'language', but both are fundamentally human – and so linguistic – methods of arranging those activities necessary to animal survival.

6. See, for example, Williams's *Keywords*.

7. The concept of 'work' as labouring activity (not its artefactual products – e.g. 'ironwork'), and at the same time its glorified autonomy, appears for the first time in Western nineteenth-century culture. At the same time the construction of the bold, autonomously confirming 'self' reaches an apogee. Within this, the questioning of the construction emerges. Freud's analysis lays the foundation for an articulated, rational disruption of the autonomous self; yet when he defined 'character types', Freud operated within a construction of autonomy as the achievable ideal of selfhood.

8. An interpretation of Freud's 'good producer' as a *worker* – but of the 'work' as an autonomous and not exchanging activity – is supported by his discussion, in *Civilisation and its Discontents*, of 'psychical and intellectual work' as the most secure 'technique for fending off suffering' since here 'the instinctual aims . . . cannot come up against frustration from the external world' (1969, pp. 16–17).

6

Definitions of Comedy

My argument that the label 'comedy' most usefully characterises a text which predominantly offers itself as 'joking' entails
action which is comic being produced in its aspect as
language; and that perception can be discovered within some
of the definitions traditionally applied to the genre. Howarth
cogently summarises two connected characteristics that have
traditionally been ascribed to 'comedy': first, that 'one of the
clearest distinguishing features of comedy seems to be its lack
of that metaphysical dimension which is of prime importance
when we come to define tragedy' (p. 1); secondly, that 'if
comedy is a form of drama whose subject matter is limited to
the affairs of this world, a further step towards our minimal
definition would be to say that its protagonists are – unlike the
heroes of tragedy – nearly all of "middling fortune" ' (pp. 2–3).
As Howarth goes on to demonstrate, such definitions of
comedy's 'middling' subject matter and setting reach back to
Aristotle (and hold the critical field until twentieth-century
critics begin to identify a very particular type of 'metaphysical', mythic import in (especially Shakespeare's) comic
drama). There is an easily apparent *ideological* connection
between the two assumptions Howarth notes: aristocrats (as
distinct from people of 'middling fortune') are more engaged
with important issues – or the issues aristocrats are engaged
with are more important. It is assumed that aristocratic
characters more properly evoke attention to implicating beliefs
such that the language of a play is read 'through' to the extra-
linguistic 'reality' of those beliefs. Conversely, then, middling
people are more likely to be comic, and identifying comic

characters as 'middling' begins to be congruent with identifying their behaviour as non-implicating, available as a joking language.

It is true that the collation of class and metaphysical status is challenged, even from the beginning of the seventeenth century, in presentations of 'domestic' (i.e. 'middle-class') tragedy such as *Arden of Faversham*; and by the last quarter of the nineteenth century the dramatic 'Naturalism' of Zola, Strindberg and Ibsen almost explicitly exhibits its dominant reformulation: in this period it is not aristocratic birth but a capacity for inner experience which defines people as 'high' or 'low'. Then it is widely possible to present socially 'middle' and even very 'low' characters as tragic – ideologically implicating – if affective implication in them is evoked. (There remains a general assumption that socially higher people are more *likely* to experience important complex feelings – it would still be difficult to present a character with a broad Cockney accent as a tragic hero.) In terms of joking or serious implication of audiences, however, social and psychological hierarchies clearly operate in parallel to prevent the production of validated 'high' characters' actions as masterable 'language'.

Affectively implicating characters are constructed as *psychologically* 'validly high'; and so comedy's production of behaviour as masterable language is implied in another well-noted characteristic of the genre. To quote Howarth again: 'the more convincingly we are led to believe in the characters of a play as individuals . . . the greater strain we put upon the concept of comedy' (p. 5). Again this can be reversed: what is presented as lacking psychological credibility will be constructed as open to joking manipulation as 'language'.

Traditional criticism's essentialising construction of this operation can be seen in its distinction between 'tragic flaws' and 'comedic folly'. For example, we find that ambition is 'social folly' when it is represented as an aspiration to a social position of which the character is unworthy; so snobs are classically funny, from Jonson's Lady Would-Be and Dekker's shoemaker's wife, to *The Good Life*'s Margot. As we have seen, a simple and overt ambition for undeserved social status is constantly found in comic characters, from the Braggart Captain in commedia dell'arte to Captain Mainwaring; from

Hancock to Aristophanes' Trygaeus riding a dung-beetle to Heaven. Although comedies usually have happy endings, this ambition is not usually allowed to triumph. In Aristophanic 'Old Comedy', characters achieve fantastic [sic] success, but in the social comedy which supersedes it, and is regarded as comedy's modern form, discursive status norms generally prevail, and comically ambitious characters are kept low. How, then, are we to characterise Macbeth's 'tragic flaw' if not as comically failed ambition for undeserved social status? The obvious answer is that within the play, the position of 'king' to which Macbeth aspires is crucially constructed not as *social* status but as metaphysically absolute.

To define comedy as dealing with 'middle' people and 'social faults', then, actually describes the effect that a joking intention has on whatever is represented within it. Jarry's *Ubu Roi* is a parody of *Macbeth* to the extent that we understand his play in relation to Shakespeare's, but it is also a comically discursive re-presentation of its plot. Jarry's conscious point in such a re-presentation is that power is made, not discovered, amongst people – as, again, in Brecht's *Arturo Ui*. Humanist critics' difficulties with Brecht spring in large part from their failure to recognise the comic element in much of his work, because they take on board his deeply serious intentions. Therefore, they assume, he must finally be interested in individual psychological experience; they applaud his work where they find this and condemn its failure where they do not. But Brecht's understanding that dominant groups manipulate metaphysical 'truth' to legitimate their advantage leads him to much comic presentation, because what is funny is – in that moment – *mastered* as language. Language is made between people, so that though discursive 'values' are difficult to alter, at least – unlike metaphysical ones – they fall within human competence. This, of course, has 'serious = important' implications.

It is perfectly possible for texts to be unserious (= funny) and serious (= important) at the same time, as are many of Brecht's and (for example) Dario Fo's and – at a less ambitious level – Alan Ayckbourn's. All these examples also contain seriously implicating moments, and some mixture of address is so common in joking texts that a definition of 'comedy'

which points *only* to its funniness must be so restrictive as to
be virtually useless. By considering the effects of their joking
presentation as central to comic works, however, we can
formulate the further effects of admixing different sites of
implication. On this basis we can redescribe the terms
traditionally used either to categorise distinctions within an
overarching genre of 'comedy' (see Gurewitch, Introduction)
or to distinguish it from other, apparently similar, genres
(Meredith, *passim*).

Those texts which are wholly without implicating elements
invite us to treat none of its representation as 'important'; and
so they do not give us the feeling that the discourse we have
mastered is itself very important or masterful. The term
usually applied to such works is 'farce', which can be
identified through its concentration on multiplex linguistic
misuse, especially the mis-speaking of social codes, but is
constructed as having no extra-linguistic reference: unlike
'satire' or 'parody', it does not imply that there *are* 'stupid (and
dangerous) people who talk like this' but only that 'anyone
who talked like this would be stupid/inept/irrational, etc.'.
In consequence farce is very exhilarating, it offers total mastery
of all the languages it represents, but it does not construct that
mastery as important in itself. Farce, therefore, has either been
evaluated by critics as trivial, or valorised through being
identified with the promotion of physical energies which are
strangely metaphysicalised (see, for example, the section on
'Farce' in Corrigan; Bermel; Caputi).

If a text does have implicating elements, but these are
mainly unpleasant (like Brecht's), the 'mastery' we have
confirmed is weakened by the presence of threat in what is
real beyond this language (thus while Brecht's later plays
imply that dominant values are conventions that can be
altered, he also demonstrates the physical power wielded by
those whose interest lies in maintaining them). In this case
none of the terms associated with 'comedy' feels quite
appropriate, because the linguistic mastery gained where we
laugh constitutes an analysis, but only a small step towards a
solution, of the problems we experience as real. Taken in
isolation, though, what is funny in Brecht could well be
described as 'irony' – as in the opening scene of *Mother*

Courage, where the recruiting sergeant has 'lost faith in human nature' because those he is tricking into joining the army run off with his money.

As a textual strategy (rather than an isolated figure of speech) irony might be defined in terms of its use of jokingly 'mistaken' language to point to something implicatingly 'wrong' in the world outside language. Irony can index more or less important wrongness: 'lovely weather' in a downpour is 'ironic' to the extent that it points beyond language, to the real weather, as undesirable; Swift's 'Modest Proposal' that the starving Irish eat their infants had more profound intentions. While irony locates that 'wrongness', whether grave or trivial, outside language, its linguistic 'mistake' is simply a recognisable reversal: for example, what we understand as bad is spoken as good. The line between 'irony' and 'satire' might be drawn in terms of irony's reversed, 'improper' speech being located in the text (it is the 'author's' speech), while pointing to some extra-linguistic wrongness.

In contrast, what is labelled 'satire' points to an extra-linguistic, real referent, but one whose 'wrongness' is constructed in terms of their *own* inept speaking – especially of social codes – while also understood as having effects that matter – i.e. intend to implicate a given audience: Pope's *Dunciad*, for example, constructs the literary standards it attacks as important. Thus Brecht's sergeant is, I think, offered as a fictional construct – Brecht's target is not the character, but the system his dangerous absurdities exhibit; the problem with the implied actual people who lie behind the sergeant is not that they 'mistake' language – as Pope's targets do – but that they *manipulate* it. Parody also constructs a speaker who is located outside the text, and may be constructed as a *very* inept speaker, but the more a text feels parodic rather than satiric, the less its 'improper' speaking is constructed as having effects that matter.

Generic labels have real but limited uses: they help prospective audiences to assess what works may offer them, they help critics to place texts. They may also promote analysis, as the grid I have been defining (whatever terms are used within it) demonstrates that funny characters' 'inept' speaking may or may not be implicatingly linked to some real

– and wrong – state of affairs; that it may or may not be 'the speaker' who is constructed as extra-linguistically real; and that what is 'really wrong' can be more or less important. I would suggest that the more a work feels like a comedy, the more its evocation of mastery is confirmed over an extra-linguistic, implicating reality that is constructed as important. Thus what are most generally accepted as 'comedies' without some privative or qualifying distinction are texts which are predominantly joking but also have strong implicating intentions which, unlike those of irony and satire, are finally cheerful. This, of course, is where the power of comedy inheres, for the status quo-affirming 'happy endings' it shares with other genres are produced in conjunction with the discursive mastery of joking. Comedies 'say' that the world beyond their language is good, *because* the language we have mastered in laughing at its inept use can – and should – prevail.

The obvious point at which a comedy text characteristically becomes implicating lies in its happy ending. This part of the play (or novel) is serious in the sense that we do not find those actions of the characters which constitute such closure funny. It is not, of course, serious in the sense of being sad. There will often be a solemn moment – in the most typical comedy closure of a wedding, this will often be the 'pledging of true love' – but a happy ending moves the audience out of their joking understanding while usually creating a buoyant imagination of future pleasure in the fictional world.

The languages comedy represents are produced as arbitrary, but this is not disturbing because we are allowed the imaginary play of our genuine transgressions and – more empowering – the strong subjectivity of our collusively marking them. However, as I suggested above, even more empowering is the sense that this constructed subjectivity can be carried over into effectiveness in the world beyond language; this happens when implicating elements are introduced without damaging – or being damaged by – the joking ones. I have suggested that works with grim implications do not feel like comedy because they limit the mastery of joking; on the other hand, what have been labelled 'black comedies' may be those where serious implication is evoked, but *damaged* by the joking – for example Orton's slapstick with a corpse's glass eye. A successful joking text must therefore steer its audience in and out of serious implication; control the degree and balance of optimistic and pessimistic judgements it offers about the actual world beyond the performance; and manipulate the connections Audiences experience between its implicating and joking elements, so that its final effect is achieved. We can see why cheerful implication, introduced in the final sequence, is the most probable closure to a comedy.

Implication with characters will probably be produced at the *end* of a joking text because it is more logical (if not more realistic) for people to move from 'error' into 'truth'. Characters who have been the object of laughter do very often 'see the error of their ways' during such closures (Caliban, in the final scene of *The Tempest*, declares: 'I'll be wise hereafter and seek for grace. What a thrice-double ass was I to take this drunkard for a god . . .'). The other satisfaction of placing implicating elements at the end may be obvious: here the audience negotiate their passage back to attending directly to the world, and if the strong joking subjectivity is finally produced as compatible with social as well as Symbolic agency, then the effect is rather like being given a doggy bag so that you can take your empowerment home with you.

Happy endings create (or maintain) exhilaration as opposed to funniness, which will also obviously be deeper if no other affect is in operation – so the more characters who are happy, and not eliciting sympathy or fear, the better. The specific event representing a happy ending is very often some version of a feast – even where a wedding forms the proper resolution to erroneous exchange of women, a feast is usually entailed – and we can understand this partly in terms of that plot simplification whereby everyone can be included in a feast. Furthermore, projected feasting also mediates between marked Symbolic error and orthodox signification, because it represents a socially legitimated transgression. Individuals eat more than they have 'earned', disrupting the discourse of exchange, and also associated with feasting is the drinking which leads to intoxicated, taboo-transgressive behaviour; but all this is permitted, *within* social codes, on this purpose-built site. Thus both the fictive characters and the audience are smoothly returned to the realm of 'proper' language by way of an event at which it is correct to be erroneous.

Thus it is the happiness of the characters, in the simplest sense of the word, which characterises these comedy closures. To identify them with various formulae of 'resolution' or 'reconciliation' is to define comedy in terms which actually apply to many texts that are uncontestably not comic; but the common belief that a comic ending is more resolved than that of a tragedy indicates, I think, the particular reconciliation which is effected by this genre: between the audience's signifying structures and the world outside language.

Howarth's clear summary of the critical tradition concludes that 'a happy ending . . . [is] of all the attributes which help define comedy . . . perhaps the most univocal and least disputed' (p. 6).[1] Many modern discussions of comedy as a literary genre (i.e. as an 'art form') nevertheless involve an implicit – and often an explicit – redescription of this as a particular kind of ending completing or constituting a particular plot structure, which in turn defines the genre: the characteristic then claimed as separable from and more profound than 'mere funniness'. A consideration of such redescriptions begins to move our attention from the nature of comedy to its effects and to the way some criticism masks its effects, which is the topic of the final part of this book. It seems appropriate in this chapter, however, to examine how some definitions of comedy respond to the operation I have identified, while – for whatever reason – they lose sight of the distinctive joking presentation of the genre.

It is misleading and also wildly inaccurate to identify the protagonists' social reconciliation, survival, or even fertile efficacy with the 'essence of comedy'. No drama could more clearly present a surviving hero reconciled with a newly flexible, re-energised 'society' than *The Oresteia*, in whose culmination Orestes is pardoned and the avenging Eumenides are transformed into benevolent guardians of Athens. Frye in fact says that 'the Aeschylean trilogy . . . proceeds to what is really a comic resolution' (1948, p. 79); but the Greeks, from whom we take the terms, definitely distinguished this as a 'tragedy' from another kind of drama: comedy. If specifically 'fertilising' heroes are demanded, *Parsival* becomes the epitomal 'comedy': if *Parsival* is a comedy, we need another term for a lot of plays. In both these examples, and in most classic tragedy, it is much more explicit than in most comedy that a widespread change for the better has occurred in the world of the play. Renaissance tragedies also conventionally end with a rightful king in control of their whole society, and modern thrillers often close with the replacement of weak or corrupt authorities by men [*sic*] of integrity. Comedy's cheerful feasting and wedding may include reformed or reinstated 'wiser' authority, but its happy ending often forms a *local* resolution to the plot's discursive mismanagement – Theseus 'overbears' Egeus's will in the disposition of daughter Hermia; he does not say that he will repeal the 'cruel Athenian law'. Comedy typically 'renews' its world *less* than unfunny texts.

However, since the *resolution* of comic endings may strike an audience more forcefully than that involved in the finales of tragedies – because the pattern whereby comedy characters achieve a 'seriously' *cheerful* ending yields a satisfying weight, as well as an invigorating optimism, to the structurally demanded closure of the texts – a mood of celebration (as opposed to a plot structure of regeneration, resolution, or anything else) appears to be genuinely connected to joking texts.

The importance of final celebration appears in the 'rule-testing' exception of situation comedies, whose individual episodes must always avoid total closure; however, when they do construct total closure, offering a final ending to a series, resolutions similar to those of discrete dramas appear: *Sorry!* finally closed with Timothy escaping his overprotective mother, who has found a willing substitute, while Timothy and his fiancée sail away in a hot-air balloon; *Hi De Hi*'s holiday camp was literally closed, and the whole cast gathered to sing 'Good Night Campers'; in the last episode of *A Very Peculiar Practice* the innocent and sincere young doctor becomes head of the practice; *Only Fools and Horses* 'closed' with the wedding of Del's younger brother, his paradoxical 'child' – including a moment of pathos as Del is shown sadly contemplating a lonely future – but later disposed of the wife to allow a further series. These patterns, then, do not distinguish 'high' from 'popular' comedy, as is sometimes claimed; they are characteristic of all funny texts, but what it is they celebrate, and what critical redescriptions instate as a cause of celebration, may bear investigation.

Comedy occupies a position in the structure of traditional literary discourses which is precisely parallel to that of 'female' in gender constructs: comedy is the 'different', lesser, subordinate genre: credited with forces not intrinsically possessed by the centre, but allowed as valuable *from* the centre. The valorisation of such aberrant qualities is typically connected with unusually allowed jubilation and/or the observance of sacred or taboo rites: with 'celebration'. In particular, comedy has been associated with the female characteristic 'fertility'.

This involves a double sleight of hand. First, its subject matter is respoken: comedy is rarely concerned with having babies; it is concerned with having women – and that more often in the sense of negotiating marriage than of copulation. True as it is that marriage often leads on to breeding, the human urge for sex is quite a distinct sensation from that of wanting or caring for a baby. To claim, for example, that 'the great symbol of pure comedy is marriage by which the world is renewed' (Helen Gardner, reprinted in Lerner, p. 249) involves selecting and respeaking the characteristic contents of the genre such that its discursive effects are reproduced as contact with apolitical and intrinsically desirable forces. The conflation of child-bearing and vitalistic urges that 'we' all share suppresses the patriarchal masculinity of discursive power, including that of the subject position of traditional criticism. Its literal masculinity is evident in remarks such as Eric Bentley's, proving that farce does not really prompt infidelity because 'our wives may be with us leading the laughter' (reprinted in Corrigan, p. 198). More problematically, traditional criticism adopts that position of discursive authority which in patriarchy is constructed as masculine: the rational and all-knowing centre *from which* what is defined as non-rational may be accorded value.

Thus, secondly, the exhilarating empowerment which comedy does offer in fact maps on to what is culturally *masculinised*, on to 'potency', but the potency comedy evokes in its audience, through its joking operations, is discursive, not biological. Given this, we can see that the relentless and

unremarked masculinisation of 'the comic protagonist' demonstrates the undeniable connection between the empowerment
that comedy does offer and the masculinisation of such
empowerment in any patriarchal society.

In the last words of *The Dark Comedy*, J. L. Styan quotes
Blake: 'I must create a system or be enslaved by another man's'
(p. 299). It seems ironic that comedy – which, if I am right,
operates through discursive collusion – should be widely
celebrated as a site on which 'the individual' escapes the
constraints of 'other men', and consequently of the inevitably
shared systems of language. But I have also argued that the
crucial effect of joking is to produce a brief 'mastery' of those
systems; and that it therefore, of necessity, occludes its
operations. On the extended scale of a comic text, the
implicating happy ending is part of that occluding mechanism,
because its effect is a wide and exhilarating empowerment.
There is a difference, though, between establishing that
comedy ends with celebratory feelings and agreeing that it
should be only and unreflectively celebrated.

The difficulty of defining comedy springs not only from the
diversity of work that can be included in the category but also
from the very evident potency of such texts. Successful
comedies elicit an immediate and evident engagement from
their audience, and more than any other 'definable' genre they
produce – as 'comedy' – a distinct and predictable effect: the
pleasure and empowerment of the funniness of joking. To
analyse this can never be a neutral project, for every
redescription or explanation, including my own, must involve
assumptions about the nature of texts, of audiences' actual
experience, of the relationships between the two. It is my
impression that the criticism of comedy is a site on which the
assumptions a critic makes about what is valuable and
possible in our general experience become especially apparent,
and in my last chapter I shall examine that criticism and
consider the projects it supports, in the context of the political
effects that I identify in all joking.

Note

1. Arguably, there are exceptions to the rule that comedies end
   happily: *Volpone* is the most notorious example. If, though,

Volpone himself is accepted as a 'comic villain' (in the sense suggested in Chapter 4), his harsh destruction is more acceptable. Perhaps it is his near success in sexually possessing another man's wife that makes him – unlike, for example, Subtle and Face – too 'dangerous' to remain at large and – unlike, for example, Justice Overdo – too 'bad' to be reformed.

PART THREE

The Effects of Joking in the World

Introduction

Because discourse is potent, its control yields power; because joking intrinsically constructs a mastery of discourse, it always has unambiguous political effects which are produced on the back of its psychic operations. Michel Foucault said that 'psychoanalysis teaches us that discourse is the power which is to be seized' (quoted in Rice and Waugh, p. 221). In this part I want to consider how joking is implicated in this seizure.

So far I have used the term 'discourse' specifically to distinguish 'language-in-use' from abstractable formulations of signifying systems, with the stipulation that 'language' always actually occurs as an activity. My reference to Foucault raises the question of the broad designation of the term, stretching from all the events that are people signifying to one another – i.e. the activity of speaking, as in linguists' 'discourse analysis' – to specifiable registers, for example 'academic' or 'scientific', to the those often unarticulated complexes of vocabulary, tone and subject matter which function like macro-dictionaries to delimit how, in a given society, it is possible to produce language. Foucault's work, in identifying major discursive structures in Western culture, has highlighted the relationship between such fundamental (and so largely 'invisible') constructions, and the possible modes in which subjects can come to know themselves as such – for example as moral or as sexual 'beings'.

I am not proposing 'joking' as 'a discourse' in any Foucauldian sense, but rather taking it to be a mode of meaning which negotiates both psychic and cultural restraints;

while its use always flavours any communication, this is less because it utilises a 'dictionary' of forms (as does a register like academic discourse) than because it manipulates the social relationship of the participants. However, joking, precisely because it offers immediate individual psychic pleasure, is very likely to be at the service of entrenched social power.

This argument can be considered, first of all, along the same lines as the debate about liberating and/or oppressive effects of 'carnival'.[1] 'Carnival' involves the inversion of symbolic hierarchies – so that what is 'high' and 'low' in terms of social status, bodily regions and other norms is reversed – but on an 'allowed site' such as special days of the year like carnival itself or the old festivities of Twelfth Night. Such sites can also be specified but non-calendric occasions, such as 'Tarts and Vicars' fancy dress parties; or particular cultural locations of which social joking and comedy performance may be seen as examples. Since it breaches norms, all carnivalesque behaviour, like joking, involves a sensation of release and a mood of rebellion; it has been argued that its operation fundamentally calls into question the 'normality' of Symbolic hierarchies, revealing them through its inversion as arbitrary constructs, not eternal truths.[2] However, its appearance only on sites which are permitted by the culture which is operating these hierarchies as norms leads us to see carnival's long-term effects as constraining rather than liberating.

This is, first, because carnival may deflect and exhaust energies that might otherwise be employed directly to oppose hierarchical dominance; secondly, and more subtly, because carnival, in inverting symbolic hierarchies, also reinscribes them: to create a socially low person as 'King for the day' in fact assumes that a ladder of social advantage is an eternal truth, and its 'carnivalesque' nature asserts that this embodiment of the ladder is incorrect. As modes of social signification, carnival and joking are virtually identical, and so are the most evident effects of both on the ideological systems of political control with which they are involved. (Foucault's work also reminds us that all discursive constructs function simultaneously to constrain individuals and to provide a site on which their limitation can be contested.)

Carnival and joking diverge, though, in that the former

occurs as participatory enactment, while the latter's activity is linguistic exchange. In carnival, a man might dress as a woman; in comedy performance the male actor in female dress is not himself immediately behaving carnivalesquely; rather, the transgressive *character* is produced, between the authorial position and the Audience, as a site on which transgressive language is incited and marked.[3] What is 'like' carnivalesque behaviour is, in all joking, pretended or imagined and attended to as utterance. Occasions of actual carnival may, then, promote rebellious behaviour in that the internalised lines restricting it to the permitted place and time can prove too weak: historically, carnivals have often ended in rioting.[4] Whatever carnival's long-term effects of deflection or reinscription, its participants define themselves in its moment as oppositional. On the other hand, because its transgressions are attended to as linguistic constructs and their marking as such is intrinsic to the experience of joking pleasure, all jokers construct themselves as *discursively* central.

Particular joking often targets actual people, and it can then have the manifest political effect of 'de-grading' power that they hold, which will be oppositional or oppressive depending upon whether the target stands above or below the jokers in the social hierarchy. But joking always constructs discursive power, and in this sense its operation is always political – quite separably from its possible involvement with 'high' or 'low' targets.

Notes

1. This is cogently explored in Stallybrass and White's Introduction to *The Politics and Poetics of Transgression*.
2. This is the argument of Bakhtin, whose work on carnival is the principle source of its exploration as a mode of signification. It is also the argument developed in relation to joking by Mary Douglas (1968).
3. The actor is, of course, part of the performance's total 'authorial position' because he is producing his performance of the cross-dressed character as an utterance.
4. See Stallybrass and White, Introduction; and, for example, Le Roy Ladurie's *Carnival in Romans*.

7

The Ownership of Language

If we consider social joking in action we can see that it immediately claims discursive space for the Teller, who is allowed to violate the normal turn-taking conventions of conversation and, literally, to 'talk more'. We can also see that this avenue to discursive power is conventionally appropriated by patriarchy's dominant group – McGhee cites several other social scientists to support his conclusion that 'the most obvious difference between male and female humor is that a male is more often the joke teller, whereas a female is typically in the position of reacting to humor' (1979, p. 201). In parallel with this distinction of actual activity, we find that the general capacity to produce and to receive joking – the possession of 'a sense of humour' – is conventionally constructed as a male attribute. Regina Barreca cites instances ranging in time from Congreve's 1695 'I have never made any Observation of what I Apprehend to be true Humour in Women' to Blyth's 1970 '[women] are the unlaughing at which men laugh' (pp. 3–4). As late as 1966 an American psychoanalyst could publish, in a major academic journal, an article discussing *why* women have 'an inferior sense of humor'; his 'evidence' for this 'fact' consisted of an earlier psychoanalyst's assertion that 'humor is a masculine trait' (Zippen, quoting Winterstein).

This ancient absurdity is more challenged at present than it has been in the past, but it persists, and this exhibits the extent to which the capacity to joke is connected with possession of that 'proper' language which commands full subjectivity, for it is that full subjectivity which patriarchy consistently denies to women and, by extension, to its other abjected groups: blacks, gays, Jews, and so on. Such groups will simultaneously be denied the capacity to make jokes and also form the conventional targets of jokes.

All habitual joking – recurrent patterns of who makes jokes and who is joked about – will both reflect and create patterns of power. Another of Foucault's important insights into the relationship between 'discourse' and 'power' is that the latter operates not as a monolithic holding of dominance and exercise of oppression, but in a complex network of negotiations: 'the manifold relations, the open strategies, and the rational techniques that articulate the exercise of *powers*' (1987, p. 6; emphasis added). It is in such a complex and dynamic negotiation that the 'political' effects of joking are involved. Studying jokes made about each other by workers in a factory, the social anthropologist Lundberg concluded that this behaviour:

> defines and re-defines the differentiated social groupings, reinforces the ranking of group members both within and between groups, and clarifies the status of one group to another. (p. 27)

So on a wider scale we can see conventional joking negotiating the accepted characterisation and positioning of groups within society as a whole. The most persistent and widespread joking targets are, evidently, most generally constructed as 'low', and joking plays an important part in maintaining that positionality.

On the macro-scale of conventional joking we see the operation entailed in every joking exchange. Jokers first of all constitute themselves as 'proper speakers' and so as the properly powerful; when the joking has targets, these become the objects of the joking subjects' speech, and the jokers take upon themselves the right to define the *nature* of their objects: Butts are definitionally lower than, more discursively inept (often in specific ways) than, and above all *different from* Teller and Audience. Sometimes someone tells us a joke that makes us laugh, even though we recognise that its target is illegitimate; this is embarrassing. The mechanism of the joke has produced a genuine and marked transgression, and our embarrassment registers the distinction between the collusive discursive empowerment that shared joking creates and the conventional social abjection of targets which may be – often imperceptibly – produced on the back of this psycholinguistic operation. It is this 'double action' which makes the politics of joking so difficult, because subjective empowerment is involved in all joking, and that is not an intrinsically bad thing. Yet at the same time, power over discourse is socially as well as psychically potent, and the fact that joking always constructs both kinds of power is demonstrated in the efforts made to restrict it.

Not all joking involves conventional targets and we can, of course, make every effort to avoid and challenge directly offensive joking. As an object of analysis, though, joking usefully exhibits the allocations of discursive power of which the masculine appropriation of humour is one demonstration. By examining conventional targets in social joking, we can see how the construction of jokers as 'proper' speakers operates reciprocally with the construction of targets as 'inept' speakers with particular 'weaknesses' – e.g. the 'mean' who 'refuse the discourse of exchange' – so that actual groups are conscripted in all societies to occupy that space (in England, Scots and Jews are mean). However, this is not the position into which women are constructed in patriarchy, in general and in conventional joking: women are not 'inept' speakers but, at a fundamental level, speechless, and joking conventions display this very clearly.

The specific nature of these conventional constructions is exhibited in joking when the precise concepts involved in the 'signified' of the targets play a part in a joke's mechanism. For example, a joke about 'a Scotsman who was asked for ten pence for a cup of tea, and said he'd have to see the cup first' works much better than the same joke told about a Zulu, for the conventional association of meanness with Scots helps us to make sense of the mechanism's puzzle; we reproduce this when we 'get' the doubled signification of 'asking for ten pence for a cup of tea'.

The English construct the Scots as mean, the Welsh as buggering sheep and the Irish as what is usually called 'stupid'. This last construction, though, is something more than simple stupidity, and it is one of the most ubiquitous constructions of joking targets. The sociologist Christie Davies lists thirty-four examples of this pattern of 'jokes told about the stupidity of some other group', covering every inhabited continent: North Americans joke about 'Pollacks', Colombians about Pastusos, Iranians about Rashtis, Nigerians about Hausa; as Davies says, these jokes 'have a near universal popularity' (in Durant and Miller, p. 45). Davies's project is the discovery of some material circumstance which will explain why particular ethnic groups occupy this 'Irish' position in relation to others. Yet the persistence of this pattern, which does not appear only between ethnically distinguished groups, suggests that it is a necessary construction which *some* group will always be identified as occupying.

Davies points out that in all cases the target groups are:

> very similar . . . to those who joke about them. For the joke tellers, the butts are the closest and most familiar of their neighbours, the most remote and provincial of their own people, or long-established and half-assimilated minorities. In general their relationship can be described as one of centre [jokers] to periphery [Butts]. (p. 45)

An additional factor Davies notes is that target groups tend to speak what is constructed as an 'inferior' version of the same tongue as the joking group, either as a second language (immigrant groups, like the Poles in North America) or in a dialect form, as the Irish speak English. We may note, though, that 'Irish'-type jokes are not usually concerned with literal 'bad speech'; they do not turn upon mistakes of grammar or pronunciation except where this, occasionally, allows some symbolic transgression: for example, Davies quotes 'how to speak Irish in one easy lesson – say very quickly "WHALE: OIL: BEEF: HOOKED" ' (p. 58). This joke is funny in inciting an Audience to say or think a taboo word, and the ineptness, which is displaced on to 'the Irish', lies in their 'ineptly' producing *unmarked* taboo language. Yet this is not in fact a typical Irish-type joke, for as I discussed above, these usually turn much more strongly on the Butts' display of 'rationally ir-rational' behaviour.

I also suggested that this is the most fundamental of joking incompetences because it generates directly what lies behind all other joking transgressions: a violation of the rule that we should *think* properly if we are to operate in the Symbolic Order. If it is 'ir-ratio-nal' to produce excess signifiers across one semantic space, the epitome of this is to produce the very construction 'rational' and 'irrational' on one site.

Thus I suggest that it is not any socioeconomic positioning which determines the constructions of groups as 'Irish-type' Butts, but rather that these Butts form a construct which joking demands: that of 'near neighbours' who are like 'us' in being able to use language (*per se*) but whose incompetence in the Symbolic Order reciprocally defines 'our' own power within it. The fact that a particular group is elected to fit this bill makes the joking more effective, because like the Scot's meanness it becomes a recognisable characteristic that is helpful in 'solving' jokes which name that target. The English know what kind of puzzle to expect when it is an 'Irishman' who was 'given cufflinks for Christmas and then had his wrists pierced' – an action that is grotesquely irrational but just possible to hold as also 'rational', and so funny, because of the similarity between cufflinks and earrings.

Beyond ethnic distinctions, groups produce Butts at local levels – different departments in offices, villages and towns that are close to one another. Clearly joking is working here to reinforce the constant operation whereby 'we' construct our identity by distinguishing ourselves from 'them'. Where superior intellect – greater Symbolic competence – is involved, these local Butts are within the 'Irish' pattern. The campus where I work currently houses two types of student, those studying for BA and those studying for BEd degrees. The BAs are the numerical minority, but constructed by both groups as cleverer and more sophisticated. Each group jokes about the other, but the BEds make jokes involving the falsity of the BAs' claimed discursive power (e.g. that they talk about incomprehensible things they do not really understand), while the BAs construct the BEds as incompetent thinkers on the Irish pattern: a student poster advertising a theatre performance warned: 'Be There or B.Ed.'.

It is almost a commonplace of feminist criticism now that

women are constructed as inferior thinkers whose speaking is incompetent – it is described in pejorative terms as 'nagging', 'gossiping', etc.;[1] it has also been noted that the ancient assumption that women 'talk more than men' – which is empirically false – reflects a radical prescription that women should not talk at all.[2] In parallel, we find that in conventional joking women do not occupy the 'Irish' position of inept speakers, but function in joking almost exclusively as objects of male sexuality. 'Woman' (and other female-determined terms) conventionally signifies 'sexual object', not 'a person', to such an extent that these terms can rarely be used in jokes that do not involve penile sex.

Conventional constructions of abjected groups can be explored in joking by 'testing' which groups can be inserted, successfully, into which jokes (like swopping 'Zulu' for 'Scotsman'), and I would suggest that the following joke-versions do not 'work' properly.

> An Irishwoman was allowed one request before being exiled in the desert, and she said she'd like a car door, so that she could roll down the window to get some air.

> Why do Irishwomen go about in threes? Because there's always one that can read a bit and one that can write a bit and one that likes to go about with intellectuals.

These are perfectly efficient 'Irish'-pattern jokes (and their funniness is, of course, overdetermined), but stipulating an Irish*woman* retards their operation because the gender of the Butts operates as an excess element. Jokes work economically: every factor that is opened is also, in good jokes, involved in their punchline's closure. For example, the joke about the 'very tall Irishman who could never find a blanket long enough, until he cut the top off one and sewed it on the bottom' works efficiently even if it is not heartily funny; whereas a joke about 'a very tall Irishman who quite liked the Forth Bridge but wondered where the other three were' does not really work (even if its pun amuses) because in the latter, unlike the former, the Butt's height is irrelevant. In the same way, the female gender registers as redundant in the two examples above – and, I think, in any possible example – while the male gender's constructed 'neutrality' is clearly exhibited.

It is possible for women to function as 'inept thinking' Butts when sexuality is involved – as in a long joke involving an 'Irish girl' [sic] whom a BBC producer tries to seduce with the offer of broadcasting on the radio, and who then treats the penis he produces as a microphone. The 'ir-rationality' of mistaking one unfamiliar object for another which resembles it in shape but is actually very different makes this a typical 'Irish' joke; but the additionally transgressive imagination of fellatio that the punchline incites 'uses up' the Butt's femaleness. 'She' is 'de-graded' not only as stupid but also in committing an action conventionally regarded as humiliating.

The female body is again involved in this joke:

> Paddy could never remember which of his shoes went on which of his feet, until one day a mate at work said 'Look, Paddy, I can help you. I'll write "R" in one shoe, so you'll know that's your RIGHT shoe, and I'll write "L" in the other and that's your LEFT one.' Paddy was delighted with the new system, and he ran home and told his little Mary all about it. And she was delighted too, and she said, 'So that's why all my knickers have got "C & A" written in them.'

The specific pun on the chain-store label could work only with female genitals, which is the most obvious reason for 'Mary's' gender. Yet the two other characters, even here, are male. We may further note that I have never found a man or a woman – including myself – who produced 'clitoris' to solve Mary's 'C': although it is topographically the best solution. In slang, and as an implicit production of joking, the clitoris, which is of no 'use' to penetrative sex, remains absent, unlike all other primary and secondary sexual characteristics. Similarly, the sex act is almost always signified as 'penetration'; jokes about women masturbating almost always deal with substitute penetration – dildoes or cucumbers: i.e. women masturbating is signified as lacking a male, not as satisfying themselves.

Many jokes about women use signifiers which construct them as attached to male partners: girlfriends, wives and mothers-in-law. In most of these, the 'inept Butt' is actually the male who cannot control his woman properly – typically, in her either denying him the sex which is implicitly his right, or taking power.

An example of the former is a joke used by Trevor Griffiths in *Comedians*: at the zoo, a wife falls into the gorilla's cage, the gorilla 'gets on top of her' and she cries in terror: 'George, what shall I do?' To which he answers: 'Tell *him* you've got a headache.' We may note that there is no need to specify that the gorilla is male, that the gorilla then signifies an aggressive creature (which gorillas are not), and also that considerable hostility is expressed towards the 'woman'. The mechanism of the joke is the equivocation between gorilla aggression and marital sex, both of which, by implication, the wife resists. The 'de-graded' figure is partly then the wife, who has claimed a false power in refusing sex and is 'justifiably' punished for it; but the punchline turns on recognising that the man is unable to obtain sex from his wife, and the male figure is consequently 'de-graded' from his position as a proper man.

Thus men who fail to control women are comic objects, while women who refuse male power are treated pejoratively – and refusing sex is a refusal of male power. Hence jokes about women lacking male sex, and about their 'really' wanting it, whilst claiming not to: as in rape jokes. These often employ signifiers such as 'nun' or 'spinster' which signify that the woman has *in general* refused male sex, while the joke involves negating the validity of that refusal. In comedy texts, female characters who refuse sex/male attention may be expected to 'really want it', from the ladies of *Love's Labour's Lost* to the nun Marguerite in Peter Barnes's *Red Noses*:

> I'm supposed to be raped! What of the raping, spindle-shanks?
> I was promised marauding prickmen. There'll be atrocities, they
> said. Rape and ravaging, they said. I want to be first. (p. 24)

(Rape jokes, of course, also perpetuate the inaccurate association between rape and male *sexual* pleasure.)

In comedy texts the characteristic of 'refusing sex' and general hostility to men is also connected – as implicitly in the gorilla joke – with 'nagging': both appear as a female falsely claiming power over men. The epitomic instance is the 'Shrew'

Kate – compare *Fawlty Towers*'s Sybil, who dominates Basil, implicitly refuses him any 'due attention', but flirts with male guests (e.g. with 'Mr Johnson' in 'The Psychiatrist': Cleese and Booth, pp. 189–296). Fierce spinsters turn out 'really' to have had sex (often built into the plot via their thus engendering the hero – Figaro's revealed mother, or 'Earnest's' Miss Prism) and then soften. Fierce 'elderly' women soften towards attractive men – as the pantomime Dame typically does towards 'the Squire' – and this leads back to the 'funniness' of women who actively pursue men, again a 'mis-speaking' in taking power. In both comedy texts and jokes the pursuing woman's 'wrongness' is often emphasised by her construction as not attractive to men, too old or too ugly – 'old ladies' who paint have a long history as figures of fun; while *The Road to Hawaii* exemplifies the classic joke: natives lead Bob Hope towards a caldron of water which the audience knows is a bath. 'Don't boil me alive! Don't eat me', cries Hope. 'You're not going to be eaten, you're going to be married', says a toothless female attendant. Hope scrutinises her and yells: 'Eat me, eat me!'

It is comically 'wrong', however, for any woman to pursue sex, as the signifier 'nympho' in popular joking suggests. An interesting example is the mildly comic figure Irma in *Mildred Pierce*, who is constructed not as physically unattractive but as 'offputting' because while she desires men (we gather), she is not ingratiating to them. More simply, in Mel Smith's *The Tall Guy*, amongst the undesirable women who contrast with the desirable heroine, one is hugely sexually demanding. She (or rather her legs) appears in flashback crying 'Pump me, pump me, Mr Petrol', while the hero performs sex with an unhappy expression. Later, in a restaurant, her 'impossibility' is confirmed (as the hero's face registers) when she offers to tell him a 'secret': 'I am not wearing any underwear.'

In these jokes, as in all instances of funniness, the meaning effects are overdetermined. Psychologically, women who nag, or refuse, or sexually demand can all be seen as 'threatening' and the male involved is constructed as a Butt in his inadequate masculinity – the Woody Allen filmic character is a clear example. This, however, is founded on a construction of 'proper', potent masculinity, as are all the apparently 'feminist' jokes about men with small willies. Men desiring women are not comic characters, even when they are 'old', unless the implication is that they are not 'up to the job', like Chaucer's Merchant's January, or Castruccio [sic] in *The Duchess of Malfi*, or the elder Steptoe, who is a 'dirty old man': i.e. these male characters are funny because they are degraded from the properly potent masculine construction they affect (Falstaff's sexual desires do not constitute one of his intrinsically comic characteristics). The distinction between the constructions of 'male' and 'female' remains, then, in that no position of any kind of 'potency' is available to women. Indeed, the vocabulary decrees that women, by definition, are 'impotent' (and being fertile is *not* the same thing).

Thus most joking does not constitute women as 'Irish-type' *inept* speakers, against whom a 'right speaking' identity can be defined. All their 'speaking' is a false claim to power which must be resisted and 'de-grades' any man who lets them get away with it. In this respect, women are constructed in most popular joking in a similar way to the term 'nigger'. Consider, for example, the joke: 'What do you call a nigger with a gun?' 'Sir!' The mechanism is the by now familiar pun on 'What do you call . . .?', but the energy of the joke comes from the implicit transgression of calling a 'nigger' by a respectful term. That the joke would not work well using 'an Irishman with a gun' demonstrates, I think, the distinction between the 'inept speaker' construction and the 'low/not-person' construction. Compare 'What do you do if an Irishman throws a grenade at you? – Take the pin out and throw it back. – What do you do if an Irishman throws a pin at you? – Run, he's got the rest of the grenade in his mouth.' Here, the stupidity is the mishandling of the grenade, which 'we' would not commit, though we imagine it (in making sense of the joke) and then mark it as 'wrong'. In the 'nigger with a gun' joke, the mistake is committed only by the jokers – both in 'mis-taking' 'What do you call . . .?' and in giving a respectful response to 'a nigger' – and not displaced on to the target figure. I suspect that the 'gun' joke's pattern could work with 'a woman', because it assigns its target *false*, not 'inept' discursive power; but the grenade joke would be inefficient if it named 'an Irishwoman' and barely comprehensible if it simply named 'a woman'.

There is one category of jokes which epitomally concerns women without necessarily involving sex or any specific relationship to a male: jokes about bad driving. This is the exception which in the proper sense of the term tests, and proves, the rule; for driving must, then, be very deeply related to exercising masculine potency, and that potency is radically allied to discursive production, so that women cannot be allowed as doing it properly.

The construction of women as non-speakers is exhibited and dynamically reproduced in joking, just as joking's operation to construct discursive ownership is demonstrated by patriarchy's denial of its competence to women. Discussing the implications of Freud's use of Jewish jokes in *Jokes and their Relation to the Unconscious*, Sander L. Gilman points to the persistent claim made by German philosophers like Buschenthal and Weininger that Jews and women 'are devoid of true humour' and elucidates the significance of this:

> true humour is thus a central matter of the difference between self and Other. It is a mode of truthful discourse which Jews and women [it is claimed] cannot possess. (p. 188)

The whole argument of this book has been to show *why* 'humour', which is apparently marginalised, nevertheless operates as 'a mode of truthful discourse' which is crucially implicated in a construction of full person-ality. To be able to joke is to be able to speak 'properly', to be a 'proper' person. In fact, it is perversely self-contradictory to assert that one does not, oneself, possess a sense of humour. The centrality of this capacity to share marked discursive aberration appears in the priority accorded to a sense of humour in selecting partners: in Lonely Hearts advertisements, for example, or the characteristics that Janice Radway found readers desiring in the heroes of popular Romances (p. 77). This, I think, is more than a search for optional 'fun'; it is the need to have one's own full discursive capacity recognised by a person who is him or herself properly competent. Thus the masculinisation of that quality, which has been questioned but by no means yet eliminated, is important and indicative.

The connection between joking's appropriation of language

and patriarchy's appropriation of joking may finally be demonstrated in relation to a style of speaking (as opposed to 'silence') which is conventionally constructed as 'feminine' and is consequently intrinsically funny. But it is not so much to women, who are already degraded, that this is jokingly allotted, but to 'feminised' men.

The style of speaking commonly regarded as 'feminine' can be shown to be related to the power that speakers of either gender feel themselves possessed of in a given discursive situation.[3] Women's speech typically demonstrates the apprehension that they have to work harder to gain attention by using redundant exaggeration, repetition and emphasis, and by naming their hearer; and seeks continual reassurance that they *are* being attended to by using 'tag questions'. Thus something like 'Darling, this is so amazingly *difficult*, isn't it?' might be regarded as a typically feminine speech. Consider, then, the joke which says that you need 'two hairdressers' to change a light bulb, 'one to change the bulb and one to say "Gary, that's absolutely *lovely*!!" ' The energy of the joke is the attribution of homosexuality to the males whose 'gayness' is indicated by stereotypically 'feminised' speech. Male homosexuality – constructed as 'improper/impotent' masculinity – is the one quality I know which it is intrinsically funny to imply in a joke or attribute to a textual character; in popular joking, male homosexuality only and always means effeminacy, and any 'female' behaviour in a male implies homosexuality. As well as in their speech patterns, female people often reflect their experienced lack of power in physical mannerisms such as touching their face or hair, which are 'comfort gestures' reflecting a need to reassure themselves; and women typically offer the world a more 'pleasant' facial expression, involving smiling and a raised brow, in contrast to the male's characteristic slight frown. These 'feminine' characteristics frequently appear in male characters who are supposed to be comically gay.

Male friendships which can be read as implying a homoerotic relationship are not intrinsically comic even when they occur in comedy texts (as in *The Merchant of Venice* or *Twelfth Night*), presumably because 'friendship' is a strong characteristic; but implications of effeminacy (like John Inman's salesman character in *Are You Being Served?* or Larry Grayson's stage persona) are constructed as very funny. It is similarly comical for a straight male character to be caught accidentally in some feminised action – admiring himself in a mirror, or tripping to land in an 'embrace' with another man. Men in women's clothing are comical, whether a male in drag plays a female character (like the pantomime Dame) or a male character is forced into women's clothing through the mechanisms of the plot (as in *Charlie's Aunt* or *The Merry Wives of Windsor*).

It is not simply that cross-dressing or implied deviance from a prescribed sexual norm is funny. Women dressed as men are not intrinsically laughable (as an 'opposite dressing' fancy dress party will always demonstrate) unless they overtly seek to take up masculine power; and the transgressive sexuality of lesbianism is virtually absent from popular joking. In terms of gender, the 'near neighbour' from whom the patriarchal man must 'other' himself seems to be the homosexual man; this appears in the general popular construction of gays as 'fluffs', 'poofters' or 'pansies' – i.e. as *weak* men – and in their comic construction as the site on which 'female' characteristics are constituted as laughable.

It is possible even for sophisticated 'ideologically sound' joking to reinforce these deeply rooted patterns of male and female power – for example, the joking about 'men's little willies' which is based on the construction of 'proper' masculinity as large-willied, so that a lack in that area is comically degrading. Cartoons such as those produced by the 'Biff' team often present a speaker who is comically, ineptly power-seeking in using pretentious, often jargonistic, language; and this is undercut by the spoken or 'thought' response of another character:

A: It's not you – it's just that I'm a genius, I have to have my space.
B: [*thinks*] What a bozo.

In this cartoon, set in a restaurant, the first speaker is a man and his respondent is a woman. Again, I believe, the joke would seem odd if the genders were reversed. If the woman spoke and the man silently mocked, the effect would be like a

Les Dawson joke: the woman would be constructed as illegitimately using powerful language, and as not paying proper attention to the male. People who enjoy Biff cartoons would probably not find that funny; but though we resist the overt sexism of such constructions, it remains difficult to accord a represented 'woman' the basic discursive authority in which comic ineptness can inhere wholly in the particular utterance, and not in the intrinsic transgression of a female speaking.

In the face of this, what strategies of resistance are available? One avenue would seem to open along the lines of accepting the identification of the Symbolic domain with masculinity and celebrating another mode of speaking – valorising the production of non-Symbolic language as a way of 'speaking' a non-patriarchal identity.[4] Luce Irigaray, for example, declared:

> there will always be a plurality in feminine language. And it will not even be the Freudian 'pun', i.e. a superimposed hierarchy of meaning, but the fact that at each moment there are always for women at least two meanings, without one being able to decide which meaning prevails, which is 'on top' or 'underneath', which is conscious or repressed. (p. 65)

One thing which this description of allegedly 'feminine' language clearly demonstrates is that joking is indeed an effect of breaching Symbolic Law – in the kind of language that Irigaray describes, where the 'Aristotelian' rule of one meaning to one semantic space is effaced, there could be no joking.

But as a matter of fact, we do joke – that is, people like me, who are women, and people who occupy other subordinated positions. Also, in my experience, people explicitly opposed to patriarchy are no more or less likely than anyone else to make and to enjoy jokes. There is, however, an argument – somewhat parallel to that of the *'écriture feminine'* position regarding language in general – that there is such a thing as specifically 'female' humour.

Certainly, since women's experience is socially different from men's, some comic contents and targets are likely to hold more female interest.[5] This, however, is a different matter from the claim that women operate an essentially distinctive *structure* of humour. Barreca, for example, believes that 'women's comedic writings depend on the process, not on the endings', and that:

> this sets the work of twentieth-century women writers apart from their male counterparts. According to Gilbert and Gubar, while male writers were exploring their disturbance at the breakdown of traditional structures, women writers were 'expressing exuberance' at precisely the same phenomena [*sic*]. . . . The absence of a "normal" happy ending – as defined by the traditional critics of comedy . . . – does not signal that the work is not a comedy. Far from it. As Cixous writes:
>
> > there is a nonclosure that is not submission but confidence and comprehension; that is not an opportunity for destruction but for wonderful expansion . . .
>
> What so often has appeared as submission is really refusal. What has been seen as solemnity is really the heartfelt, limitless nature of women's laughter. (1988, p. 17)

The confident exuberance of this position is attractive, but it has problems. For one thing, there is a sliding between the 'openness' of a text's total structure and an undetermined relationship between signifiers and signifieds. Barreca claims:

> [women] write comedies that deflate the language of the symbolic order. . . . Comedy is a way women writers can reflect the absurdity of the dominant ideology while undermining the very basis for its discourse. They can point to the emperor's new clothes. The creation of non-sense, puns, language play associated with eradicating the boundary between the imaginary and symbolic reaffirms that women's use of language in comedy is different from men's. (p. 19)

But 'non-sense, puns', etc. are *funny* when their transgression of 'the boundary between the imaginary and the symbolic' is marked, so that those boundaries are reinscribed; the unmarked use Irigaray describes would have nothing to do with definable 'comedy'. Furthermore, their use can hardly be appropriated to female or even to oppositional writing.

Nor, I think, can it be claimed that an openness of textual structure is 'female', though it can reasonably be argued that open texts disrupt audience expectations. Discourses which disrupt audience expectations at the level of language-use, textual structure or content may well function as oppositional strategies in certain circumstances. Women are likely to be in the forefront of this, as of other oppositions to patriarchy, because we are the people most consistently oppressed by patriarchy. Still, there is no reason or use in labelling it, in comedy writing or elsewhere, *essentially* feminine. Without entering the long and ancient argument about whether 'open' texts are inherently oppositional or inherently elitist, or depend upon their content for their political effects, a particular and essentially political effect may be implicit in the disruption of comedy's characteristic happy ending: the refusal of such closure could be seen as preventing the movement which installs 'proper' speaking of its represented social codes back into the implicating actual world. While no such structural distinction can be made amongst the operation of *joking* – of making things funny – which must always, by definition, affirm the psychic Symbolic Law, the possibility of a distinctively oppositional *comedy* form 'opens'.

Something similar is suggested by Susan Carlson (1978) in relation to Caryl Churchill's *Cloud Nine*. The first Act of the play farcically subverts conventional gender codes, taken at an extreme in colonial Africa, through the characters' wild 'misbehaviour' coupled with the performers' stipulated cross-gender casting. The second Act moves the action forward one hundred years (to 1980), makes the characters twenty-five years older, and casts all but one to same-gender performers; also, 'the tone of the second act is completely different from that of the first: farce modulates to a gentle, thinking comedy of words, characters and predicaments' (p. 313). In this way, Carlson points out, Churchill is able to represent the confusion *and* empowerment which follow from trying to live beyond the stereotypes foregrounded by the first Act's farcical disruption of them. The audience is neither returned to established order nor left merely raging against it. And Churchill is able to provide a final 'happy ending' beyond this exploration, when the female performer playing Betty in the second Act embraces the male performer who played her in the first: a resolution within the actual presentation, and not the represented world.

Comparing *Cloud Nine* with *Comedians*, *Laughter* and *Not Waving*, Carlson says of their authors: 'Churchill goes one step beyond [Trevor] Griffiths' and [Peter] Barnes's and [Susan] Hayes's preoccupations with comedy by defining for comedy a new, constructive relationship with the rage comedy orders for us' (p. 315). 'Rage' characterises the response of those for whom the established orders do not work – a feeling arguably vented in conventionally closed comedy and left working, but not to any positive end, in wholly open texts. In identifying Churchill's capacity to harness oppositional outrage without deflecting it, Carlson does not (as her counter-examples show) make her gender an issue. Barreca, on the other hand, raises serious problems by insisting that her argument proves 'that women's use of language in comedy is different from men's' (p. 19).

I cannot see any empirical grounds for asserting that *all* women and all men write in certain, distinct ways, in comedy or elsewhere. All my own experience – in addition to the very fact that societies put so much effort into ensuring that girls and boys are different – suggests to me that no behaviour is essentially gendered which is not immediately necessary to biological reproduction. I would argue that if women produce or enjoy texts of any kind whose concerns are not typically male, it is right to assert that these works are not less important or interesting for that reason; just as characteristics like co-operation and flexibility, socialised more strongly in most women than in most men, should be recognised and valued. Still, the line between celebrating qualities tradition-ally fostered, ascribed and downgraded as 'the feminine', and asserting that they are *essential* attributes, remains a fine one. It must be trodden carefully, or descriptive celebration will become a new version of evaluating prescription (are unco-operative women, however irritating, not 'real' women?).

There is also the danger that in celebrating what we achieve despite or even because of our subordination, women will embrace that subordination as 'essentially' theirs. That seems to be the enormous danger of the '*écriture feminine*' analyses of differential language-use.

The question of feminist responses to Lévi-Strauss, raised in Chapter 5, is relevant here. Cowie, like other critics she quotes, adopts a construction of women as *binary* signs which is not implicit in the anthropologist's formulation. Binary signs or symbols, as I discussed, are discursive entities which have stable designations. The distinction between analysing the sign 'woman' and analysing women *as signs* is not academic because it confuses what is discursive and so contingent – changeable no matter how deeply installed – with the non-discursive, which is not. Male people could theoretically be used as much as females to perform exchanged kin identities, even if they never have been. Representations of males *do* mobilise Symbolic significances as much as representations of females do, albeit usually different ones. It is easy and dangerous to slide from describing women's discursive privation to analyses which essentialise and thus prescribe it.

It is logically coherent to argue that if language-use is acquired in relation to the recognition of sexual difference, sexually different people will acquire differentiated uses of language; but the extreme implications of the claim that rational language 'belongs' to crested people are horrendous. It means that cloven people must *all the time* be silent, or irrational, or in schizophrenic bad faith. Obviously, the last would apply most of the time, because women go about most of every day using rational language. It is palpable nonsense to suggest that anyone, of either gender, could or should 'do without' rational language most of the time; given this, the essentialised ascription of non-rational language (and therefore thought) to females is as absurd and damaging when it is apparently celebrated as it was when it was used to deny women the vote.

If language is the field of full human subjection, no section of humanity can own it, no matter how long or how radically they appropriate it. We should not collude with patriarchy's appropriation of the Symbolic. Since all joking generates its power and pleasure through constructing Symbolic competence, women (and all abjected groups) need to lay claim to it, while at the same time our own experience of ideological deprivation may help us to use its potency carefully. Although it is not easy, we have to explore the difference between individual and hegemonic empowerment, and between what is psychically necessary to all 'human being' and what is ideologically constructed as 'masculine' and 'feminine'.

Every human being *needs* to use language most of the time *as if* signifiers and signifieds were immovably stuck together across identical semantic spaces, while the unstable arbitrariness of the connections erupts into everyone's language-use. It is clear that ideologies of dominance, however, must insist upon language's stable closure in order to construct the 'absolute' values which legitimate domination. It is also clear that such values, operating sociologically, are extended upon the back of psychic desires to which they offer Imaginary (in every sense of the word) satisfactions. This in itself points to the central presence of instability in all linguistic operations, which continually generate the need for such satisfactions. What is not yet clear is how we can disentangle that internalisation of the Law which produces subjection – and in my view is a necessary condition for any meaningful human being – from its contingent formations around the ideological absolutes of the prevailing culture.

Elizabeth Grosz concludes her 'Feminist introduction' to Lacan:

> [t]o utilise Lacan's insights without being ensnared with them: this seems the task for those feminists interested in analysing and theorising subjectivity. A cultivated ambivalence may help to sustain the arduous and pleasurable task of reading Lacan: and the more tedious but productive task of criticising and moving beyond his position, creating from its remainders a new kind of account of subjectivity that grants women autonomous positions as subjects and objects of knowledge. (p. 191)

(I would add that feminists of either gender should be interested in analysing and theorising subjectivity, because while the oppression of women – at least as much as other subordinated groups – is 'in the final instance' a physically enforced economic exploitation, the abjected subjectivity patriarchy extends to women is the root at which it produces and reproduces itself. If that were not so, such a patent absurdity could not endure.)

I have based my analysis of joking on Lacan's account of subjectivity, whilst noting his unacceptable phallocentricity, because it offers an account (and not just an assumption) of the inextricable connection between using language and having identity, which finds identity contradictory because language is contradictory. In distinction from Lacan, I identify the pleasure and power that all joking yields in its temporary resolution of that contradiction. The phrase 'the mastery of comedy' may describe the whole circle of effects to which I have been pointing: all joking 'masters' discourse, and thereby seizes ideological power and constructs and confirms socio-economic power. The very separation traditional criticism has made between 'joking' and 'comedy' enacts an operation of discursive power whilst masking the distinctive discursive power which the pleasurable funniness of comedy affords. And in patriarchy, the power of joking significantly supports and is appropriated by 'natural' male authority. This clarifies but does not solve the difficulty of women joking.

What I have tried to show so far in this chapter is the extent to which joking and comedy are *likely* to support constructions of 'the male' as the fully subjected owner of discourse: either by directly affirming them or by reinscribing them through apparently oppositional inversions. Because it must operate tacitly, joking must confirm what Teller and Audience 'already know'; it always confirms the collusive identity of the Teller/ Audience group as those whose knowledge and competence constitute 'proper' thinking. It is therefore very unlikely radically to change an Audience's perceptions, and we are all of us deeply saturated with a constructed 'knowledge' of masculine dominance which is thus implicated in our performance of Symbolic competence. But at the same time, many of us know that we deny patriarchy's validity; and the socially confirming operation of joking holds just as good for oppositional as for dominant elements of identity construction. Since joking is hugely overdetermined, there is more than one reason why most things are funny, and getting a joke will have more than one effect. Joking happens in actuality, not in theory, and each particular instance of joking and of comedy will have particular effects in relation to its context, its content, and their interactions. I am sure it is a mistake simply to insist that these are all 'for the good', but it would be just as simplistic to insist that they are always repressive.

Again, it is possible, as Churchill's *Cloud Nine* shows, to produce comedy which challenges the basis of social codings and explores living with different ones as a real possibility. Just as repressive ideologies often operate by tiny 'snowflakes' of effects that build to huge drifts of constraint, so many small inroads will shift them.

Furthermore, while (even for those who want to oppose it) the Symbolic hierarchies of patriarchy lie deeply piled upon the fundamental psychic structures without which it is impossible to 'make sense', reality exceeds all its representations. Encountering a person who is female, for example, involves more than encountering the signifier 'woman'. Thus I think the rise of the female stand-up comedian, if it continues, must be both a sign and an agent of change. Even if the stage persona and/or the content of her jokes can be seen to be conservative, a woman is present as the originator of joking discourse.

At the beginning of this book I pointed to the joking of young children and signing apes to support my contention that the use of discourse intrinsically involves the capacity and the desire to joke. It does not 'eradicat[e] the boundary between the imaginary and symbolic', it breaches it to release its tension but also to reinscribe it. I do not think we can be human without that boundary, and the pleasure and power of overruling the Law which subjects us cannot be denied, although they are ideologically appropriated. But just as joking exhibits the extent of representation's effects, so it demonstrates their limits. Discourse makes sense through representation, but it is not *itself* a representation, it is an actuality. In actuality joking can – and sometimes does – confirm relationship and identity beyond the miserable limits of patriarchy.

Notes

1. See, for example, Dale Spender's *Man Made Language* which, despite criticism of its 'essentialist' view of speakers, remains a

trenchant summary of how 'women' and 'language' are typically constructed in relation to each other.

2. See, for example, Coates's summary of assumptions (pp. 31–4) and of experimental verification of masculine verbosity (pp. 97–103).

3. See Coates, pp. 112–14.

4. For summaries of such approaches see, for example, Moi (pp. 89–173); Cameron (1985, pp. 114–33).

5. The performance artist Bobby Baker presents pieces centred on cooking which I have seen move most of the women in an audience to delighted laughter, while most of the males remained stoically perplexed. Work like this valuably articulates our distinctive experience and offers social solidarity. The more widely known domestic concerns of Carla Lane's television comedies (*Butterflies*, *Mistress*, *Bread*) have been acclaimed for the same reason, though with less cause; for here the problem certainly remains, as in 'willy' jokes, that a funny presentation of the feminine situation is likely to reinscribe it unchanged. New signifying systems like Baker's performance art, not yet fully co-opted to patriarchal ownership, make texts *less* recuperable by it. For this reason several feminist artists (Hannah Wilke, Catherine Elwes) have chosen to use it, not necessarily comically. Although it is unfamiliar at present, this work is not always inaccessible and may be one site where comic mastery can be appropriated by women.

Masking the Effect
Literary Accounts of Comedy

Joking makes us feel good, so we want to feel good about joking. On top of this, literary criticism is posited on the project of encouraging its readers' appreciation, even when it does so by categorising some productions as not to be appreciated. It is not surprising that the literary criticism of comedy has always valorised at least some section of the genre. However, the many versions of 'true' comedy and its 'value' have functioned to occlude considerations of its intrinsic discursive and so political effect. This is especially the case in the 'mythological' strain of twentieth-century comedy criticism.

Until around the beginning of the twentieth century, laughter is generally treated as a response to other people's 'minor' faults, and comedy as a display of these. One consequence is that localised events rather than literary structures form the focus of attention, so that in such moralised readings the 'happy ending' of a comic text is simply assumed to represent completion of the comic characters' 'correction'. A problem quite readily apparent in these accounts lurks in a great deal of comedy criticism: the 'we' who dissociate ourselves from 'faulty' comic characters are regarded as a pre-exisiting, not discursively constituted, unified group. The position of the audience is assumed to be singular, their interest in what constitutes 'good society' identical, the correctness of their views an absolute given, not a constructed confirmation. Within these approaches the ideological effectiveness of comedy is clearly indexed, but not treated as a dynamic process requiring interrogation; and since comedy is quite as likely to degrade simple 'foreignness' or sexual 'deviation' or female power-seeking as it is to castigate greed or meanness – since, as I have tried to show, it largely constructs the categories of behaviour it subsequently disavows – interrogation of *what* a comedy 'corrects' is necessary before we applaud it.

It was not, however, a refutation of sociopolitical bias which brought about literary criticism's rejection of moralistic accounts as central to the understanding of comedy. The early twentieth century produced in many areas a reversal of that automatic valorisation of 'society' and 'civilisation' which is implicit in the moralistic accounts of comedy; but this was replaced by a new set of unquestioned, unitary values rather than a view of values as the products of discourse that are differentially advantageous to different people. In fact the absolute value of 'society' is directly inverted, to produce the absolute value of 'individuality' as something in every sense 'prior' to society. The individual's 'natural' life, far from being the 'nasty, brutish and short' experience of which Hobbes and the Enlightenment saw civilisation as the saviour, becomes a self-evident ideal; and the Romantic excellence of our primal human being is eventually found (through a late-Victorian scientisation of its expressions) to be epitomically liberated from oppressive communal conventions in 'comedy'.

The construction of humanity's deepest truth as something potentially, or even inevitably, diminished by society seems to be as attractive to the twentieth-century mind as the opposite assumption of civilisation's inevitable superiority was to past centuries. However, since this construction treats 'society' as a universal phenomenon and its members as sharing the same interests as much as the earlier assumption (paradoxically, individuals are identical in their uniqueness), it still evades questions about how particular social norms restrict particular sections of societies. So it is worth investigating its history and its especial mobilisation in relation to comedy.

On the one hand there is the track of thinking which attends directly to joking or 'humour', and comes to locate *all* laughter as *valuably* involved with energies that are distinct from social convention (compare the distinction between decorous and indecorous laughter that Sidney in the sixteenth or Meredith in the nineteenth century made with Langer or Corrigan). A particular strand of this thinking approves 'joking' because of its connection with 'creativity' in general, as in Koestler's *The Act of Creation* or, more recently, Jonathan Miller (in Durant and Miller, 1988); but its most influential origin lies in Bergson. His *Le Rire* (*Laughter*, 1900) promotes a 'vitalism' whose opposite is 'mechanical life'; this clearly stems from the same impulse as the Romantic rejection of industrialised 'civilisation', but Bergson, still using a 'corrective' model, sees 'mechanistic' behaviour as the object of laughter, which thus opposes it. Although the importance of Freud's *Jokes and their Relation to the Unconscious* is generally admitted, his work tends to be recruited as an exponent of vitalism, because his 'unconscious' is equated with 'the natural' and the inhibitions he shows joking overcoming are conflated with civilisation's undesirable restraints (see also Henkle); or he is criticised for ignoring laughter's 'natural energy' (see Michael Neve, 1988).

Crucially, the energy laughter embodies is treated as an entity in its own right. 'Humour' is thus persistently identified with a force whose lyrical celebration as potentially disruptive, vitally [*sic*] necessary yet finally unspeakable directly parallels constructions of spirit beings in other cultures. More precisely, it parallels Western accounts of those constructions, which have been 'discovered' as re-presented in comedy texts. Even the most academic discussions of 'humour' consistently produce a mystification, a species of mythologising, which in itself enacts the thinking that comes to be critically associated with 'comedy'. For example, Walter Nash, in *The Language of Humour* (1985), declares, with rising rhetoric, that it is:

> more than an amiable decoration on life; it is a complex piece of equipment for living, a mode of attack and a line of defence, a method of raising questions and criticising arguments, a protest against the inequality of the struggle to live, a way of atonement and reconciliation, a treaty with all that is wilful, impaired, beyond our power to control. (p. 1)

The other track of thinking attends to the genre of 'comedy' rather than to 'laughter'. It reflects a very similar philosophy, but focuses on plot and character structures which involve the successful struggle of individuals against social restrictions. The undesirability of these restrictions lies not in socio-economic oppression but in 'sterility', and what is *funny* in comedy becomes a secondary expression of the 'fertility' the genre allegedly celebrates. Comedy is attributed an essen-tialised, metaphysical significance as asserting the triumph of life over death, while its usual social setting is acknowledged in formulations whereby the hero's energies 'revive' his society. (No contradiction is seen in the masculinity of most major characters within a genre that extolls fertility.)

The moralists' correction of faulty individuals by the good society is potentially totally reversed. However, Northrop Frye put these two positions together, and (using the term 'humorous', like Plato, to mean 'not self-knowing') found 'the essential comic resolution' in an ending where 'the normal individual is freed from the bonds of a humorous society, and a normal society is freed from the bonds imposed upon it by a humorous individual' (1948, p. 76). In the context of the ideological project – not just of comedy but of literary criticism too – we may note the unreflective use of that potent term 'normal'. But this is not, for Frye, the full story:

> [t]he ritual pattern behind the catharsis of comedy is the resurrection that follows the death, the epiphany or manifesta-tion of the risen hero. . . . Thus the resolution of New Comedy [by extension, *all* comedy after Aristophanes] seems to be a realistic fore-shortening of a death-and-resurrection pattern, in which the struggle and rebirth of a divine hero has shrunk into a marriage, the freeing of a slave, and the triumph of a young man over an old one. (pp. 78–9)

The 'argument' Frye posed in this article was soon extended in his *Anatomy of Criticism*, to which I shall return; and his account of comedy became central to the view of the genre which has proved hugely persistent, in which 'comedy' is defined, potentially separated from funniness, in terms of triumphant natural forces. These forces may well, in the redescription of comedy texts, be connected with the genre's typical attention to the biological facts of life (which I have redescribed as taboo-breaking, and which involves funniness), but they are also supposed to transcend them. Suzanne Langer, for example, identified 'comedy' with any text in which the protagonist's survival can be taken to signal a general survival against the Fate which destroys him in (diacritically defined) Tragedy. In Langer's account, a concept of death as cyclically entailing rebirth, offered in terms of oriental reincarnation beliefs, is married to a Western valorisation of 'the individual', producing 'the buffoon' as the definitionally central comic character, about whom she can now reveal the truth – the buffoon:

> really is . . . the indomitable living creature fending for itself, tumbling and stumbling (as the clown physically illustrates) from one situation to another . . . he is the personified *élan vital*. ('The comic rhythm', in *Feeling and Form*; reprinted in Corrigan, 1981, p. 77)

I have already suggested that in the relentless masculinisation of comedy's 'indomitable living creatures' we are dealing with something more fundamental than the habitual use of male terms to encompass both genders. Here I want to investigate the implications of the construct which is evident in Frye and Langer, of a vital force embodied identically in every individual, which all literature – and especially comedy – proclaims. In theory, comedy's putative 'mythic structuring' is a different question from its expression of 'supra-biological energy'. In practice, the supposed mythic/ritual patterns are celebrated *because* they instance the 'natural vitality'.

As a generalised literary value, a mystified yet somehow earthy 'life force' can be traced back to F. R. Leavis and his circle, who imposed their values on the fledgling discipline of 'English Literature' throughout the middle of the twentieth century. As Terry Eagleton (1983) summarises, referring to the circle's polemical magazine, 'these values could be summarised as "Life", a word which *Scrutiny* made a virtue out of not being able to define' (p. 42). Leavis's 'Life' was not in conflict with 'true civilisation', but only with the aberrance of 'mass culture'; and such explicit academic elitism became untenable as higher education, first in America and then in Britain, widened its social market. However, if overt Leavisism is considerably out of current literary critical fashion, its influence remains substantial, not least when academics come to speak of 'comedy'. Thus Corrigan's Preface asserts that:

> there is something almost biological about the comic – and this is the source of its energy as well as its appeal to audiences. It reveals the unquenchable vitality of our impulse to survive. The central intuition of comedy is an innate and deeply felt trust in life. (p. 8)

Torrance (1978) announces that *The Comic Hero* is:

> comic . . . primarily by virtue of the festive values he celebrates and embodies; values of biological life and imaginative freedom, of dogged humanity and belligerent self-hood. (p. viii)

Roger B. Henkle's *Sewanee Review* article 'The social dynamics of comedy' identifies the relativising effect upon all values entailed in their comic presentation; but in the move that typifies so much comedy criticism he nevertheless assumes that beyond these lies an absolute and inscrutable value, which 'we' all share; in comedy:

> for a moment we become aware of the way in which the designation by a social order of what is important and what shall have most meaning for people has stultified our natural vitality. (p. 214)

Critical formulations like these are likely to produce strong but deeply opposed reactions. Some readers will find it so obvious as not to need discussion that this 'belligerent self-hood' embodying 'natural vitality' is one of the benevolent, Humanistic faces of patriarchy, and that in masking the relationship between our experiences of self-identity and our being as *a part of* society there is produced as normal, natural and unchangeably given what is in fact one particular social construct, whose unreflective celebration ignores the disadvantage it entails for many 'abnormal' individuals.

This is clearly exhibited in the conclusion to George McFadden's *Discovering the Comic*. Having worked through a definition of 'the feeling of fun or joy that identifies the comic' as arising from engagement with 'a being that is notably engaged in . . . self-maintenance, self-definition and self-sustenance' (p. 11), McFadden's final words warn:

> If the comic is to survive . . . it will outlast, in literary art at least, the present wave of attacks upon the subject and the individual personality. The most severe test of all would come if freedom should one day cease to be the most valued of human desires and goals; if, for example, a commonality of status, risk and reward should become the most valued object of human activity. (p. 254)

The explicitness with which McFadden links the essentialised 'freedom' that comedy can be constructed to celebrate to a society where 'status, risk and reward' are *not* equal may stand as an explanation to the second set of strongly reacting readers, who find an incomprehensible grumpiness in questioning such celebrations.

I have suggested that it is the nature of all joking, including comedy, to produce a very 'desirable' sensation – that of personal empowerment, which we inevitably and rightly value; but for precisely this reason it is sensible to scrutinise the full range of its effects. This 'vitalism' may then appear as an *essentialised* construct which broadly corresponds to the dynamic identity formation I have described as the operation of joking, whilst masking its discursive process. Thus while this generally vitalistic comedy criticism may sometimes identify important aspects of the genre, it needs to be scrutinised as much as moralistic accounts to discover how *far* it accurately defines the works it addresses, what social effects within those works it may efface, and what projects of its own it serves.

The same is true of the specifically mythic interpretations of comedy; but if we are to understand the full range of this criticism's effects, it must be set within wider contexts. Throughout the third quarter of this century, 'mythic' criticism predominated in accounts of all literary genres – Frye's *Anatomy* is precisely a myth-structured account of all literature. However, the discovery of 'fundamental' mythic patterns, and the identification of literature as valuable *because* it reflects them, is itself part of the far more generalised post-Romantic distrust of 'civilisation' and its rational thinking; and what began as a distinctly radical philosophy becomes involved by the end of the nineteenth century in the increasingly complex ideology which 'orders' a largely enfranchised, literate, post-industrialised society. Eric Hobsbawm describes how, after 1870:

> and almost certainly in connection with the emergence of mass politics, rulers and middle class observers rediscovered the importance of 'irrational' elements in the maintenance of the social fabric and social order. As Graham Wallas was to observe in *Human Nature in Politics* (1908) 'whoever sets himself to base his political thinking on a re-examination of the working of human nature, must begin by trying to overcome his own tendency to exaggerate the intellectuality of mankind.' A new generation of thinkers has no difficulty in overcoming this tendency. They rediscovered irrational elements in the individual psyche (Janet, William James, Freud) in social psychology (Le Bon, Tarde, Trotter), through anthropology in primitive peoples whose practices no longer seemed to preserve merely the childhood traits of modern humanity (did not Durkheim see the elements of all religion in the rites of Australian aborigines?), even in that quintessential fortress of ideal human reason, classical Hellenism (Frazer, Cornford). (Hobsbawm and Ranger, p. 268)

It is Hobsbawm's last two examples, Cornford and Frazer, who lie behind the 'discovery' of literature's mythic patterning. However, there is also a particularly English strain of twentieth-century 'mythologising', which has been widely identified and also explicitly associated with an active ideological project. Geoffrey Hartman describes:

> what, by the time of the Second World War, had become a standard British response to national crisis: the construction of long-past, green, alternative worlds of percipient peasants, organic communities, festivals, folk-art, and absolute monarchy to set against present chaos. (p. 109)

The complicity of this 'Englishness' with the rise of 'English literature' as an academic study, 'in complex implication with ideologies that were imperialist, nationalist, empiricist, sexist, elitist' (Sinfield, p. 182), has been considerably documented (see, for example, Baldick; Colls and Dodd; Eagleton; Hawkes; Mulhern). Its especial affinity with the criticism of comedy – and above all that of Shakespeare's comedies – is apparent in Hartman's vocabulary. Since Shakespeare is constructed as our iconic 'literary [sic] genius', his work must 'naturally' exhibit what is fundamental and timelessly valuable in English life.

Thus Frye's 'green place' assumes an uncontested location in Shakespeare's comedies, and Barber refers virtually as a matter of course to – for example – 'the traditional saturnalian customs . . . kept up in the *unselfconscious* regions of the countryside' (p. 16; emphasis added), or to a 'modern reader's' realisation of 'how completely all groups who lived together within the agricultural calendar shared in the responses to the season' (p. 22). However, these evocations of England's ancient rural harmony are weighted with wider significance: for Barber, for example, 'May-game wantonness has a reverence about it because it is a realisation of a power of life larger than the individual, crescent in both men and their surroundings' (p. 24); the project of *Shakespeare's Festive Comedy* is summarised as the demonstration of how it 'brings into focus, as part of the play, the significance of the saturnalian form itself as a paradoxical human need, problem and resource' (p. 15). Very similarly, Frye's comedic Shakespeare, from *The Comedy of Errors* onwards, is groping towards 'that profounder pattern, the ritual of death and revival that also underlies Aristophanes, of which an exact equivalent lay ready to hand in the drama of the green world' (1948, p. 80).

The particular strategy of associating comedy with ritual patterns is apt in that joking discourse, operating as the aberrant case whose marking defines the central field, is literally like the operation of taboo categories with which it so often deals; so that the academic mythification of 'humour' responds obliquely to a real quality in it. It can be seen, however, that the modern Western essentialisation of forces that are assumed to express themselves both in myth and in 'humour' belongs to thinking which arises and has effects well beyond the bounds of comedy criticism. Not only did this obviously influence critical interpretations of comedy; its continued currency there in turn plays a part in maintaining its wider credibility, which should be carefully examined.

Although neither its premisses nor its empirical consequences are usually spelled out, the 'mythic' strategy for deflecting the dynamic discursive mastery of comedy is wholly implicated with instating as truth the early twentieth century's version of 'primitive' society, in which people live(d) better lives through being 'more in touch with natural rhythms', as expressed in their mythological thinking. This superiority has not been related to social justice – often the opposite – and has only recently been invoked to exemplify ecological efficiency. On the contrary, it tends to evade all the implications of accepting ourselves as necessarily social, and by asserting that we are – or should be – governed by 'natural' mental patterns, it forecloses debate about how particular societies manipulate the selves produced within them.

This desirably 'natural' thinking has been variously located: in present (or recent) non-Western cultures; in the ancient conditions of Western peoples (which contemporary primitives may be taken to exhibit); and/or in a 'universal unconscious'. Even though Frye, for example, rigorously insisted on the distinction of the last from actual exemplifications ('it does not matter two pins to the literary critic whether such a ritual had any historical existence': 1957, p.109), they cannot be separated, because the 'objectivity' of the mythic patterns is dependent upon their universal appearances; and it is only as objectified (not as constructions of the critic or of the author) that they can be treated as universal absolutes.

Thus the willingness with which these patterns are still 'discovered' in comedy is related to an assumption of their objective existence. Taken in this way, they offer an immensely attractive reconciliation between 'science' and 'religion'. Yet they have no objective basis whatsoever as 'primitive' practices, and that is only one flaw in the argument for an objectively existing 'universal unconscious'. Literary critics' continued circulation of theories and 'facts' derived from the psychology of Carl Jung and the anthropology of Sir James

George Frazer, without examination or sometimes articulation of those sources, seems culpable (even if literary criticism reflects rather than influences its ambient culture). It damages the authority of literary criticism.

The assumption (as made by Frye) that particular and fundamentally valuable *contents* of the human mind are universal, and repeatedly expressed in cultural productions, derives from the 'archetypes' that Jung located in the 'universal unconscious'. The simplest argument against this is logical: even if certain patterns appear repeatedly and independently in cultural products from different places and times, that is not evidence of underlying 'archetypes' which have an existence separable from the sum of productions. You might as well claim that because rivers exhibit the same set of geographic patterns across the globe, these reflect separately existing riverine archetypes rather than repeated interplays of similar forces and resistances. At the level of scientific 'fact', any real operation of 'universal archetypes' would also entail a Lamarckian genetic transmission of mental contents, which is flatly contrary to current genetics; and of course it involves an inborn, prestocked unconscious quite incompatible with any understanding (including Lacan's) of conceptual language as experientially acquired.

However, the apparently 'scientific' nature of Jungian thought took considerable colour from Sir George Frazer's anthropology – manifestations of 'archetypes' which demonstrate the existence of the 'collective unconscious' are often authorised by footnote references to *The Golden Bough* – while Frazer's work has deeply influenced literary criticism, and especially that concerned with comedy; not only through Jung's formulations, but also directly. It was, for example, the central Frazerian construction of the ritual of 'the old king's death and the new king's rebirth' which Cornford 'discovered' as the origin of Greek comedy, supported by 'facts' whose authority is cited as *The Golden Bough*. The influence of that construct upon Frye, Barber, and beyond them a whole school of criticism, will already be evident. Yet anthropologists themselves have been showing, for more than a quarter of a century, that what Frazer and his colleagues produced were reflections of their own ideas, not accounts of other people's:

for example, the first chapter of Douglas's *Purity and Danger* and all of Kuper's *The Invention of Primitive Society* document this at length and in detail. Nevertheless, to an astonishing extent, Frazer's interpretations of present and ancient 'primitive' ritual still pass as factual accounts of 'what people do' – or did – not only in literary footnotes but as part of current educated 'knowledge'.

In *The Making of the Golden Bough*, Robert Fraser charts the construction of this fascinating but quite imaginary edifice of theory and concocted fact. Its initial move produced the concept of 'sympathetic magic' – like will influence like – as a primitive attempt at scientific control (rapidly extended by Evans-Pritchard, for example, to yield 'witchcraft' beliefs). For Frazer its particular use was an explanation of the ritualised replacement of impotent by fertile Kings, which he believed to be a common 'primitive' practice. This was amplified into the *religious* (as opposed to 'magical') ritual of the 'scapegoat', where the cast-out figure carried away the community's guilt or 'sins'. As the vocabulary already suggests, Frazer's project is in fact the 'discovery' of ancient patterns within which the Christian redemptive sacrifice will be located. He sought evidence for this in Western civilisation's prehistory and in (then) contemporary 'primitive' behaviour assumed to parallel that.

Any interpretation of radically foreign cultural behaviour is fraught with questions. Lévi-Strauss's structuralist anthropology questioned the validity of interpreting any isolated behaviour, in any culture, as having an intrinsic 'meaning' that can appear in separation from its relationships of similarity and difference with all other elements in that culture. More simply, faced with unfamiliar behaviour, people see what makes sense to them: a version or an inversion of their own signifying structures. Different observers will make different constructions.

In *Man on Earth* John Reader describes three accounts of the Bambuti, Congolese hunter-gathers, given by scientific travellers in the first decades of this century, all of whom spent months or years living with the tribe. Schweinfurth found them 'degenerate remnants of a declining race'; Schebasta found them a 'loathsome' people who had become the 'vassals' of neighbouring agriculturalists; Martin Johnson and his wife found 'unspoiled children of nature . . . [who] spend their days like youngsters at an endless picnic'. More recent anthropological studies have in turn identified complex ecological and social systems through which the Bambuti's survival in their forest environment is intricately linked with that of their agrarian neighbours (pp. 149–55).

Thus the problem is not just that what Frazer himself advanced only as theories have come to be treated as facts, but that the factual instances he catalogued at such length must themselves be understood as theoretical interpretations, even when he cites behaviour which certainly occurred. As Fraser shows, *The Golden Bough*'s multitudinous examples are largely based, even in their own terms, on contradictory and often blatantly unfounded assumptions not only about why something was done, but whether such things occurred at all.

Frazer never disguised the second-hand nature of all his information. We may assume that the Ancient Greek and Roman descriptions of foreign people's observances, which he used with immense erudition but inevitably filtered through his own assumptions, first reflected their original author's presuppositions and patterns of understanding. Frazer's accounts of contemporary foreign rituals were also all second-hand. In the first edition of *The Golden Bough* they were drawn from reports sent to him in response to his own questionnaires. By the time he wrote the twelve-volume third edition he was using accounts of both contemporary and ancient ritual formulated by workers who were themselves depending upon the theoretical assumptions of the earlier editions. It is not surprising that Frazer, and the informants guided by him, found what he was looking for. Wherever it has been possible to approach again the behaviour Frazer categorised, other explanations have been offered (see Douglas; Kuper). It is particularly ironic that twentieth-century literary criticism found especial parallels between Renaissance comedies and Frazer's universal primitive rites in that many of Frazer's accounts actually are Renaissance texts – sixteenth-century accounts of 'savage sacrifice' by Catholic missionaries in South America, or records of Tudor festivities which he uncritically assumes to be 'ancient' practices.

Frazer imagined a pattern of primitive thinking which would underlie and explain Christianity's crucified and resurrected God; he believed that his copious examples constituted evidence of its objective existence in other men's minds. The valency of these constructions throughout twentieth-century thought is a study in itself, and it cannot simply be 'blamed' on Frazer; yet an important part of these constructions is the 'fact' of their universal appearances, and wherever one tries to track the evidence that literary critics offer for this, it is overwhelmingly Frazer who lies at the end of a trail of footnotes and references – above all in discussions of comedy. This is true of Frye's identification of the 'ritual re-birth' structure in all comedy, with the attendant Shakespearian 'profounder pattern' of 'the green place'; of Langer's 'buffoon', Wellesford's 'Fool' and Barber's 'saturnalian pattern'. (This is not always obvious – Langer's impressive list of multicultural buffoons, for example, has one footnote reference to an unauthored and undated *Encyclopaedia Britannica* entry which – given the date of her book – must be based on Frazer.)

Works like these, which were written some time ago and depend fundamentally upon Frazer's 'facts' and/or on citations of other works in turn dependent upon Frazer, are still widely circulated with no warning that their informational content is inaccurate (see, for example, the Corrigan or D. J. Palmer anthologies of comedy criticism to which I have referred). Penguin reprinted *Anatomy of Criticism* in 1991. One still sees Frazer directly produced as an authority: rather touchingly, Bryant (who is a professor at the University of Kentucky), having constantly cited *The Golden Bough*, agonises during a discussion of *The Merry Wives of Windsor* that 'Frazer records no instance in which laundry, as such, is used as part of a ceremony' (p. 117). Works which set out to re-examine the *significance* of 'ritual' nevertheless cite Frazer in passing with the assumption that the practices he collected took place as he described them (e.g. Bristol's *Carnival and Theatre*, p. 28; Weimann's *Shakespeare and the Popular Tradition in Theatre*, pp. xx, 1).

In this way a potent ideological construction, particularly giving validity to and taking it from the site of comedy, has passed into general awareness with the apparent support of 'scientific' anthropology. If mythic patterns no longer form the cutting edge of new literary criticism, the extent to which Frazer (brilliantly, and with the intention of absolute integrity) *invented* what he catalogues has never been articulated in literary circles.

More generally, recent critical texts – including Nash's Introduction quoted at the beginning of this chapter – continue to produce the comic as a mystic, if not mythic, truth; and this is not confined to 'literary' criticism. Gerald Mast, for example, writing about film and explicitly acknowledging the importance of funniness in comic film, nevertheless does so because 'only by being successfully funny can a comic work capture human experience. And only by capturing human experience can a comic work be serious' (p. 27). Even more recently – and even more mystically – Robert Goff manages to find that in Buster Keaton's films, a storm 'enjoins a receiving and affirming of the elements', while a double-take at a rope refusing to hold knot shows 'Keaton characteristically stressing a moment of receptivity at the heart of significant action' (in Durant and Miller, pp. 106 and 107).

Its continued currency suggests that there is much at stake in this maintenance of 'primitive vitality' as humanity's 'deeper meaning' – and in constructing comedy as the major site of its expression. We have seen the identification of myth with eternal expressions of humanity's deepest energies as one aspect of an irrationalising retheorisation of all human being, and one effect of this is to affirm identity's autonomous, non-social 'nature'. Additionally, whether or not its roots in the mythic are explicated, vitalistic literary criticism, specifically, of *comedy* further constructs a powerful discursive position from which no human activity seems to be excluded, yet within which all is transformed.

It can allow a deep pessimism about 'the human condition' (as in the 'tragicomic' constructions discussed in Chapter 4) that issues in no politicised or oppositional awareness, but in an 'acceptance', constructed as 'wisdom', which surely acknowledges a rooted interest in social arrangements remaining significantly undisturbed: as Corrigan, for example, concludes:

> our fate may be tragic, but comedy, in all its forms, is an

assertion of that life force which enables us to be joyous
survivors in an acceptable and accepting world. (p. 11)

Nelson's *Comedy*, published in 1990, begins and ends with the
assertion that 'if laughter is essential to comedy, the yearning
for harmony and reconciliation is equally so'; therefore:

> the most honest ending is that which simply returns us to the
> inadequacies of the world . . . to the awareness that life is a
> struggle in which nobody can always be on the winning side,
> and each of us will sometimes fill the role of victim, scapegoat
> or fool. (p. 186)

These initially appealing sentiments, so often repeated, stir
questions: who, exactly, is enjoined to find harmonic, reconciled acceptance of what? In what contexts, to whose
advantage, will such pleasant quiescence actually operate?

Humanist criticism's still dominant construction of comedy
can be seen as a central exhibition of its involvement with
patriarchy's restrictive operations, even when the critic
explicitly and sincerely advances liberal views; vitalism also
offers some particular solutions to problems that comedy
raises for the traditional Humanist 'literary academic' register.
It speaks those energetically enjoyable sensations which the
genre typically evokes in a diction that is extremely respectable; so it considerably dignifies the 'mere pleasure' which is
the genre's most obvious effect, while evading the issues of
sociological power entailed in its creation: if any adverse
effects are noted, they can be dismissed as distinct from the
universal benevolence of 'true comedy'. The construction of
the energy of comedy as an extra-individual and thus finally
metaphysical force also allows the funniness of comedy, with
all the 'low' behaviour it entails, to be accommodated within a
schema that nevertheless firmly displaces it from centre stage.
This has been explicitly, if not critically, noted in relation to
Shakespeare: D. J. Palmer's Introduction to his anthology of
criticism declares that with the advent of this critical approach,
'at last Shakespeare's comedies could be discussed, not merely
as amusing and charming yet implausible stories, but in terms

of their deeper meanings, their profounder patterns and rhythms' (p. 170).

Thus mythic vitalism, progressing from 'scientific' analyses of anthropological or psychological eruptions to a more general construction of metaphysically 'eternal' energies, allowed Humanistic criticism to accommodate an otherwise awkward site which history had landed in the domain to which it laid claim. In this way the implicating 'happy ending' of comedy, not its joking, becomes the definitional characteristic of the genre; and while insights and illuminations abound in Frye, Barber, and many other Humanist critics, as I have argued ignoring the discursive relativity of joking presentation is critically as well as ideologically flawed, since it fails to distinguish 'comedy' from other narrative genres.

However, post-structuralist literary criticism has not yet offered any major response to the peculiar nature of comic texts. Such critical writing has for a long time, of course, questioned Humanist absolutes, pointing to their discursive production and, often, to their sociopolitical effects. One result is that the capacity to unfix meaning, transgressively to unclip signifiers from signifieds, can become the value to be celebrated in any good text. Using a phrase suggestively evocative of clowning, Roland Barthes declared:

> The text is (should be) that uninhibited person who shows his behind to the *political father*. (p.53; original emphasis)

This opens towards the identification of every 'good' text with the transgressive condition of joking discourse; but with the 'marking' of transgression denied. This itself implies a certain kind of elitism, for as I pointed out above, considerable discursive confidence is implicit in the enjoyment of overtly unfixed language. It is also unrealistic: if identity is discursively constituted, some negotiation of our ambiguous symbolic 'subjection', through transgressions jokingly marked as such, will always be a human pleasure.

It is not, of course, that any postmodernist critic would want to 'do away' with joking or comedy, but that its particular operations are unlikely to be the site of their investigations. When they are, the comic remains – here as in other discourses

– a curiously slippery object of attention. Steve Neale's examination of 'Psychoanalysis and comedy' applies a Lacanian rereading of Freud's *Jokes and their Relation to the Unconscious* to the genre in film; it shares with earlier articles by Jeffrey Mehlman and Samuel Weber, to which it refers, the perception that in his formulation of 'smut' as a secondary sexual satisfaction, Freud approaches a Lacanian theorisation of the displacement of desire into discourse. But connections between discursive formations and joking (which are also suggested in Mick Eaton's article in the same issue of *Screen*) are less pursued than the discovery of a Freudian theory of discourse. Mehlman finds that 'the further we pursued our analysis of *Der Witz*, the more did the apparent object of Freud's analysis – jokes – disappear' (pp. 460–1). This is, perhaps, an accurate reflection of Freud's book; it also suggests the persistent clouds of ink that joking, as a direct subject, produces in all critical approaches.

Conclusion

'Laughter', we say, 'keeps us sane' – 'You've got to laugh, else you go barmy.' This commonplace observation echoes much that literary critics identify in comedy texts: the release from restrictions of all kinds that joking can bring, its relativising of the values that can operate to restrict us, its exhilaration. That exhilaration leads us, though, to the inescapable connection between the joyful joking we would all want to celebrate and the oppressive, belittling joking most of us would condemn. Whether we laugh at those who are socially more powerful than us or at those whom we dominate, or only at plays on words and concepts, in joking we are both breaking rules and asserting that sanity lies with us. Insanity – madness – is commonly defined in terms of extreme hallucinations or delusions about the material world, but most of us, most of the time, are not dealing with such aberrant perceptions of the *material* world but negotiating the 'rationality' of our own and others' perceptions of *social* reality. This kind of sanity is not an objective state but a position established in discursive interaction, the sum of the shifting equation of how we respond to what others say and how they respond to us. This is the 'power over discourse' Foucault says must be seized; the power Fishman defines as 'the ability to impose one's definition of what is possible, what is right, what is rational, what is real' (p. 397). This is not simply the power to speak, but the power to define what speaking constitutes 'proper' language.

Lacan's psychoanalysis suggests that all our capacity to speak meaningfully depends upon operating the basic rule of 'same and different' so that we can represent something as the signified of what we take as a signifier; and that the meaning we most fundamentally seek is also the condition of any more elaborate signification – recognition as a subject by the other who is significant to us: 'man's desire finds its meaning in the desire of the other, not so much because the other holds the key to the object desired, as because the first object of desire is to be recognised by the other' (Lacan, 1977a, p. 58).

If all our speaking in and of the world is founded on this most basic need to be 'recognised by the other', it is not surprising that our sense of personal worth, and also of what is culturally valuable, are intricately knotted up with others' recognitions of what we say and think as being 'possible, right, rational, real'. Nor is it difficult to see how ideologies, in constructing powerful groups as sites of the validating other, can manipulate our responses, so that it is difficult to feel personally valuable unless we are recognised as such from those sites. In particular, patriarchy's appropriation of 'proper' language makes it difficult for women to operate, socially and psychically, without deference to masculine superiority. These self-perpetuating patterns of seized and accepted discursive power operate, often quite unconsciously, in parallel and intersecting levels from the most intimate to the most institutional, from the most personal to the most culturally generalised. I have tried to show how joking is implicated in these patterns.

Since joking is a mode of discourse, its effects are always highly overdetermined, resulting from multiple interactions between situation and content; and since joking involves intimately shared assumptions, we are especially likely to notice its multiplicity of conditions when we scrutinise examples of it. It is precisely those intimately shared assumptions about what is discursively proper that make joking so potent. The recognition of our subjectivity that successful joking allows is deeply pleasurable, but it is achieved through establishing particular uses of language, particular kinds of thinking, as rational, without articulating what they are. Joking, therefore, can potently instate norms that are unexamined and may be harmful to other people or to the jokers themselves.

Not only does joking often involve social 'taboos', it operates exactly like taboo formations in establishing the bounds of what it is 'right' to do, think, say – through the *marked* transgression of rules. Identifying the Rule of the Symbolic Law as the fundamental prohibition joking marks allows us to see that its social potency is founded on an inescapable psychic need. The nature of that need, the 'proleptic' formation of the self in the other's response to our speaking, seems itself irrational or nihilistic unless we accept that identifying selfhood as an interactive process, not an absolute entity, remains an assertion of self as valuable and part of what is real. By directing our attention to the appearance of this process in joking we can understand more about what connects 'funniness', from tiny social exchanges to major comedy texts, and also see what an important part its pattern plays in all aspects of our lives.

Postscript
Cultural Relativity and
Joking Structures

I have offered an account of 'joking' – what happens when someone finds something funny – in terms of its involvement with our construction as subjects through our recognition by others as producers of Symbolically Lawful language. My examples have been taken from current Anglophone practices and from past texts still accepted as valuable in the West. Thus I have been referring to a culture in which the 'family group' that Lacan seems to assume as the infant's site of development does structure adult interactions with children, even in instances where they are not in fact brought up by a 'mother' and a 'father'. The question must arise, though, of how universally Lacan's formulation of the Symbolic Order might be applied, and/or how far my formulation of joking as a negotiation of it applies to cultures with relevantly different ideological formations. I do not have space to do more than indicate how this might be pursued.

It is certainly notoriously difficult to transpose particular jokes from one culture to another – jokes are often said to be 'untranslatable'. One reason for this is simply that they share a requirement of all discourse – sometimes noticed as if it were particular only to joking – that participants have to comprehend each other's signification. Nash, for example, points out that the children's joke ' "VAT 69" is the Vatican's phone number' depends upon knowing roughly what 'the Vatican' is, and that 'VAT 69' is a brand of whisky (p. 4). However, non-joking utterances – 'Do you like "VAT 69"?', say, or 'Have you visited the Vatican?' – require exactly the same competence. The difference is that joking's distinctive aim of funniness, and the intimacy it proposes, *evidently* fails if the Audience do not share the Teller's knowledge; while the failure of discursive effect that would be indexed by a response like 'I'm not familiar with what you're talking about' to (for example) an ordinary question is less stark and less damaging.

Thus joking emphasises the difficulty of translating any kind of utterance from one cultural context to another; and where the joke depends wholly upon one word form having multiple potential signifieds, the difficulty always entailed in translating from one tongue to another is manifest. Obviously, you cannot exactly translate into Hindi a possible English joke about being chased by an animal and having a 'bare behind'; but then that kind of sound pun cannot be 'translated' into the written form which distinguishes the two signifieds.

Neither of these problems, then, tells us anything about how far the kind of psychic structure I have identified in joking can be generalised.

Some anthropologists have studied non-Western joking, mostly with reference to the institutionalised 'joking relationships' that appear in some African social formations; and Mary Douglas (1968) explicitly argues that African and Western joking share the same construction and function. She finds that 'jokes . . . connect widely differing concepts' in a manner which 'destroys hierarchy and order' (p. 369). Her conclusions are compatible with my own – they have influenced them – but since she is not interrogating psychic levels of operation, it is possible to say only that they leave open the possibility of some psychically fundamental correspondence between Western and non-Western joking.

My assumption is that all language-users will play with marked transgressions of its rule, and that the basic Law of Symbolic Order must be universal (if it is true at all, it must be true everywhere); but that the construction of joking may vary to some extent, in ways that will reflect differing *ideological* constructions of the nature of language and identity. There are some obvious differences between the construction of joking in contemporary and earlier Western cultures. In the High Middle Ages, for example, the term 'comedy' was used of any story which 'introduces a situation of adversity, but ends its matter in prosperity'. (This is Dante's famous definition, in the

'Letter to Can Grande'; quoted in D. J. Palmer, p. 31.) It might be argued that a literate culture which had no textual site distinctively associated with funniness must have had a different construction of textuality, and of language itself; and medieval Christianity identified language with the Second Person of the Trinity – the 'Word' ('Logos' in the original Greek) through which, in the Gospel of St John, God created the world – while its religion was central to medieval ideology. Arguably, the more language is ideologically attached to a superhuman guarantor, the less strongly users need to internalise the 'proper' operation of its rules, and the degree to which that internalisation is demanded might relate to the amount of pleasure derived from different kinds of joking. One of the ideological changes most widely accepted as indicating the end of the Middle Ages is a splintering of accepted constructions of God and of the whole world as the Book in which His univocal meaning can be read; and a distinctive change in joking practices occurs amongst the many cultural shifts that mark the ensuing Renaissance.

Joking and funny performances certainly existed throughout the Middle Ages, but there seems to have been a preponderance of enacted taboo-breaking – illicit sexuality, physical aggression, scatological pollution – over tight verbal manipulations of 'punch-line' joking. This appears in drama, literature and in the books of 'jests' which are probably as near as one can get to socially exchanged joking: 'jests' differ from 'jokes' (such as appear in modern compilations) in recounting a story where something 'de-gradingly' funny happens to someone, rather than turning on a punchline. Punch-line jokes, like comedies with complex plots, involve Symbolic negotiation more strongly and depend upon *social* transgression less than do 'pure' violations of taboos. It would seem that – in Freud's terms – the Middle Ages required less psychic permission for 'tendentious' joking, and this was true across the social spectrum in a way that is quite surprising to modern sensibilities. The recent joking of the 'alternative' comedians which is currently found (enjoyably or scandalously) shocking would for the most part have seemed tame to courts for whom poets wrote about (for example) kissing arseholes (Chaucer's 'Reeve's Tale') or a man being pelted with eggs (Bernardo's story of the false 'friar' in Castiglione's *The Courtier*). So in the pre- (or early) Renaissance world, not only does taboo-transgressive joking seem overwhelmingly to predominate over verbal manipulation, it was most certainly accepted socially in a way that seems extraordinary to current Western expectations. These different uses of joking may relate to differing explicit ideologies and, crucially, to differing dominant operations of psychic identity formation. Perhaps in the earlier period, we are looking at a more externalised, overtly social identity formation, where the need constantly to confirm our 'proper' subjection within the Symbolic domain does not operate as such a radical anxiety, and that is why 'stories that degrade Butts' are more generally found funny than punchline anecdotes and their equivocating visual parallels. 'Play on words' seems in earlier cultures rather to take the form of riddles that are enigmatic but not transgressive investigations of their complex signification – not the 'jokes' of modern riddles.

Both comedy texts as distinct high-art practices and the social practice of punch-line joke-telling appear in Europe as a new ideology moves to dominance: bourgeois humanism. The word 'joke' does not appear in English until the seventeenth century. This period also coincides with that generally taken to produce 'the subject [as] the free, unconstrained author of meaning and action . . . unified, knowing and autonomous' (Belsey, p. 8). Belsey and other writers have developed Foucault's perception that this autonomous subject is a site of new freedoms for the individuals concerned but also involves a distinctive form of social management, whereby we are incited to know and to *control* 'ourselves' within the specific formations of selfhood that the culture produces.

Many critics have also argued that the seventeenth century's newly dominant ideology is reflected in texts where the language is predominantly 'dialogic': used 'not simply as an instrument of representation, but as an object of representation'. Such language 'lends itself to parody, to presentation at one remove, to utterance in "intonational quotation marks"; . . . and so relativises the conjunction of language and reality' (Womack, p. 7).

Peter Womack thus describes qualities of Ben Jonson's writing which reflect its historical moment of production

(Kiernan Ryan, for example, makes similar points about Shakespeare), and these qualities are very similar to the linguistic effects I have identified in joking. They will function jokingly when a marked transgression is involved; so their joking use may correspond to moments when the pressure exerted by and against Symbolic identity formation is sufficient for 'mastering' it to be deeply pleasurable. 'Dialogic' language appears in extant English literature at least from the fourteenth century (Chaucer, Skelton), and how far it operated *jokingly* for its original audience must always be conjectural; but by the seventeenth century – in Jonson, for example – it frequently appears as part of what is explicitly signalled as 'comedy'. At the same time, 'wit', which is verbal and valuable, is separated from other 'gross' forms of joking which are inferior or even despicable.

Meredith's 1877 'Comic Spirit', boasting 'the sage's brows and the sunny malice of a faun', is already presaged in Sidney's 1588 distinction of desirable 'Delight' from undesirable 'Laughter' (for useful summaries and examples of these theories of comedy, see Howarth and D. J. Palmer, which both include extracts from these texts); taboo-transgressive joking, from the seventeenth century onwards, steadily becomes less respectable, and although it is always nevertheless popular, it is progressively toned down such that what was once acceptable fun in courts is now most unlikely to appear in the 'lowest' clowning.

The development of specified social and textual sites for funniness also historically maps quite closely the institutional regularisation of language form – for example, the regularisation of 'correct' (and thus the unhappy invention of 'incorrect') spelling. The development of such external orthodoxies of form may suggest a need to impose formal stability of language-use where its internalised stability is simultaneously less certain, more 'at stake' for individuals, and more required in a society increasingly controlling its members through the 'guilt' of their minds rather than the 'shame' of their bodies. That would be one factor leading to a greater exercise of the 'freedom from/control over' the Law of language that punchline joking emphatically delivers.

There is an almost self-evident connection between the

ideological importance attached to tying signifiers strictly to coextensive signifieds, and the amount of pleasure/power derived from markedly unstringing them. Empirically, concern to maintain patriarchal order and lexical order are connected: in summer 1990 a furious debate raged in government and educational circles about whether candidates in History examinations should be penalised for grammatical and spelling mistakes: those for and against the inviolability of 'correct' wording were explicitly identified as 'politically' right- and left-wing respectively. Equally, 'post-modern' critics from Barthes to Irigaray, who describe the self as a construct, have celebrated texts and advocated language-use which 'would undo the unique meaning, the proper meaning of words, of nouns, which still regulates discourse' (Irigaray, p. 62). This again suggests that there is a systematic connection between the cultural variation that can be found in dominant modes of identity formation, constructions of 'proper' language – in every sense of that phrase – and modes of joking.

Bibliography

This bibliography has three purposes: (a) to enable readers to locate my quotations and references; (b) to clarify the provenance and first date of publication of works with which some readers will not be familiar; (c) to indicate other work in this area (for which see also Note 1 to Part One's Introduction).

Austen, J. (1956) *Northanger Abbey* [1818], London/Oxford: Oxford University Press (World's Classics).

Austen, J. (1956) *Persuasion* [1818], London/Oxford: Oxford University Press (World's Classics).

Ayckbourn, A. (1986) *Woman in Mind: December bee*, London: Faber & Faber.

Bakhtin, M. (1984) *Tvorchestvo Fransua Rable*, 1965, transl. H. Iswolsky as *Rabelais and His World*, Bloomington, IN: Indiana University Press.

Baldick, C. (1983) *The Social Mission of English Criticism 1848–1932*, Oxford: Clarendon Press.

Barber, C. L. (1959) *Shakespeare's Festive Comedy: A study of dramatic form and its relation to custom*, Princeton, NJ: Princeton University Press.

Barnes, P. (1985) *Red Noses*, London: Faber & Faber.

Barreca, R. (ed.) (1988) *Last Laughs*, New York: Gordon & Breach.

Barthes, R. (1976) *The Pleasure of Text*, transl. R. Miller, London: Jonathan Cape.

Belsey, C. (1985) *The Subject of Tragedy*, London: Methuen.

Bergson, H. (1956) *Le Rire*, 1900, transl. F. Rothwell as *Laughter*, in W. Sypher (ed.), *Comedy*, New York: Doubleday.

Bermel, A. (1982) *Farce*, New York: Touchstone/Simon & Schuster.

Bristol, M. D. (1985) *Carnival and Theatre: Plebeian culture and the structure of authority in Renaissance England*, London: Methuen.

Bryant, J. A. (1986) *Shakespeare and the Uses of Comedy*, Lexington, KY: University of Kentucky Press.

Cameron, D. (1985) *Feminism and Linguistic Theory*, London: Macmillan.

Cameron, D. (ed.) (1990) *The Feminist Critique of Language*, London: Routledge.

Caputi, A. (1978) *Buffo: The genius of vulgar comedy*, Detroit, MI: Wayne State University Press.

Carlson, S. (1978) 'Comic collisions: Convention, rage and order', *New Theatre Quarterly*, **3**, 2, 303–16.

Carpenter, R. (1922) 'Laughter, a glory in sanity', *American Journal of Psychology*, **33**, 419–22.

Carroll, L. (1977) *The Complete Works of Lewis Carroll*, London: Macmillan.

Cleese, J. and Booth, C. (1988) *The Complete Fawlty Towers*, London: Methuen.

Coates, J. (1986) *Women, Men and Language*, London: Longman Scientific and Technical.

Colls, R. and Dodd, P. (1987) *Englishness: Politics and culture 1880–1920*, London: Croom Helm.

Cornford, F. M. (1934) *The Origin of Attic Comedy* [1914], Cambridge: Cambridge University Press.

Corrigan, R. W. (ed.) (1981) *Comedy: Meaning and form* (2nd edn), New York: Harper & Row.

Cowie, E. (1978) 'Woman as sign', *m/f*, **1**, 1, 49–63.

Deleuze, G. and Guattari, F. (1977) *L'Anti-Oedipe*, transl. R. Hurley *et al.* as *Anti-Oedipus: Capitalism and schizophrenia*, New York: Viking.

Derrida, J. (1987) 'Le facteur de la vérité', transl. A. Bass in *The Postcard: From Socrates to Freud and beyond*, Chicago, IL: University of Chicago Press.

Dickens, C. (1971) *Bleak House* [1853], Harmondsworth: Penguin.

Douglas, M. (1966) *Purity and Danger*, London: Routledge & Kegan Paul.

Douglas, M. (1968) 'The social control of cognition: Some factors in joke perception', *Man*, **3**, 361–76.

Durant, J. and Miller, J. (eds) (1988) *Laughing Matters: A serious look at humour*, London: Longman Scientific and Technical.

Eagleton, T. (1983) *Literary Theory: An introduction*, Oxford: Blackwell.

Easthope, A. (1983) *Poetry as Discourse*, London: Methuen.

Easthope, A. (1989) *Poetry and Phantasy*, Cambridge: Cambridge University Press.

Eaton, M. (1981) 'Laughter in the dark', *Screen*, **22**, 2, 21–8.

Fishman, P. (1978) 'Interaction: The work women do', *Social Problems*, **24**, 397–406.

Foucault, M. (1967) *Histoire de la folie*, transl. R. Hurley as *Madness and Civilization*, London: Tavistock.

Foucault, M. (1978) *La Volonté de savoir*, 1976, transl. R. Hurley as *The History of Sexuality. Vol. I, An Introduction*, Harmondsworth: Penguin.

Foucault, M. (1987) *L'Usage des plaisirs*, 1984, transl. R. Hurley as *The History of Sexuality. Vol. II, The Use of Pleasure*, Harmondsworth: Penguin.

Fraser, R. (1990) *The Making of the Golden Bough: The origins and growth of an argument*, New York: St Martin's Press.

Frazer, J. G. (1906–15) *The Golden Bough: A study in comparative religion* (3rd edn in 12 vols), London: Macmillan; (1st edn in 2 vols, 1890; 2nd edn in 3 vols, 1900; abridged edn in 1 vol., 1922; *Aftermath* to 3rd edn, 1936).

Freud, S. (1900) *Die Traumdeutung*, transl. J. Strachey as *The Interpretation of Dreams*, in J. Strachey (ed.), *The Standard Edition of the Complete Psychological Works of Sigmund Freud* [hereafter *SE*], London: Hogarth, 24 vols, 1953–73; vols 4–5 (1955).

Freud, S. (1905) *Der Witz und seine Beziehung zum Unbewussten*, transl. J. Strachey as *Jokes and their Relation to the Unconscious*, *SE*, vol. 8 (1960); 1966 paperback edn, London: Routledge & Kegan Paul (from which my citations are taken).

Freud, S. (1908a) 'Der Dichter und das Phantasieren', transl. J. Strachey as 'Creative writers and day-dreaming', *SE*, vol. 9.

Freud, S. (1908b) 'Charakter und Analerotik', transl. J. Strachey as 'Character and anal eroticism', *SE*, vol. 9.

Freud, S. (1909) 'Analyse der Phobie eines fünfjährigen Knaben', transl. J. Strachey as 'Analysis of a phobia in a five-year-old boy', *SE*, vol. 10 ('Little Hans' in Penguin Freud Library 8, pp. 165–305).

Freud, S. (1914) 'Zur Einführung des Narzissmus', transl. C. M. Baines as 'On narcissism: An introduction', ed. J. Strachey, *SE*, vol. 14.

Freud, S. (1921) *Massenpsychologie und Ich-Analyse*, transl. J. Strachey as *Group Psychology and the Analysis of the Ego*, *SE*, vol. 18.

Freud, S. (1927) 'Der Humor', transl. J. Strachey as 'Humour', *SE*, vol. 21.

Freud, S. (1930) *Das Unbehagen in der Kultur*, transl. J. Riviere as *Civilisation and its Discontents*, rev. and ed. J. Strachey, *SE*, vol. 21.

Fromm, E. (1982) *Greatness and Limitations of Freud's Thought*, London: Abacus.

Frye, N. (1948) 'The argument of comedy', in D. J. Palmer (ed.), *Comedy: The theory of comedy in literature, drama and criticism*, London: Oxford University Press, pp. 74–84.

Frye, N. (1957) *Anatomy of Criticism*, Princeton, NJ: Princeton University Press (from which my citations are taken); Harmondsworth: Penguin, 1990.

Gilbert, S. and Gubar, S. (1986) *The Female Imagination and Modernist Aesthetic: Women's Studies Vol. 13*, New York: Gordon & Breach.

Gilman, S. (1985) *Difference and Pathology: Stereotypes of sexuality, race and madness*, London: Cornell University Press.

Goldstein, J. H. and McGhee, P. E. (1972) *The Psychology of Humor*, New York: Academic Press.

Goodchilds, J. (1959) 'The effects of being witty on position', *Sociometry*, **22**, 261–72.

Goodchilds, J. and Smith, E. E. (1964) 'The wit and his group', *Human Relations*, **7**, 22–31.

Gordon, M. (1983) *Lazzi*, New York: Performing Arts Journal Publications.

Grice, H. P. (1975) 'Logic and conversation', in P. Cole and
J. Morgan (eds), *Syntax and Semantics*, vol. 3, New York: Academic
Press.

Grossmith, G. (1924) *The Diary of a Nobody* [1892], London:
J. Arrowsmith.

Grosz, E. (1990) *Jaques Lacan: A feminist introduction*, London: Routledge.

Gurewitch, M. (1975) *Comedy: The irrational vision*, London: Cornell
University Press.

Gutman, J. and Priest, R. F. (1969) 'When is aggression funny?',
Journal of Personality and Psychology, **12**, 1, 60–5.

Happe, P. (ed. and intro.) (1972) *Tudor Interludes*, Harmondsworth:
Penguin.

Hartman, G. (1980) *Criticism in the Wilderness*, New Haven, CT: Yale
University Press.

Hawkes, T. (1986) *That Shakespeherian Rag: Essays on a critical process*,
London: Methuen.

Heilman, R. B. (1978) *The Ways of the World: Comedy and society*,
Washington, DC: University of Washington Press.

Henkle, R. B. (1982) 'The social dynamics of comedy', *Sewanee Review*,
90, 200–16.

Hobbes, T. (1968) *Leviathan* [1651], ed. C. B. Macpherson, Harmondsworth: Penguin.

Hobsbawm, E. and Ranger, T. (eds) (1983) *The Invention of Tradition*,
London: Cambridge University Press.

Howarth, W. D. (ed.) (1978) *Comic Drama: The European heritage*,
London: Methuen.

Irigaray, L. (1977), interviewed and transl. C. Venn, 'Women's exile',
Ideology and Consciousness, **1**, 62–76.

Jung, C. G.(1959) *The Archetypes and the Collective Unconscious*, in
Collected Works, transl. R. F. C. Hull, vol. 9, Part I, London:
Routledge & Kegan Paul.

Kerr, W. (1967) *Tragedy and Comedy*, New York: Simon & Schuster.

Koestler, A. (1970) *The Act of Creation* (Danube edn), London: Pan.

Kolve, V. A. (1966) *The Play Called Corpus Christi*, London: Edward
Arnold.

Kuper, A. (1988) *The Invention of Primitive Society: Transformations of
an illusion*, London: Routledge.

Lacan, J. (1977a) *Ecrits*, 1966, transl. A. Sheridan as *Ecrits: A selection*,
ed. J.-A. Miller, London: Tavistock.

Lacan, J. (1977b) 'Les quatres concepts fondamentaux de la
psychanalyse', in *Le Séminaire de Jacques Lacan, Livre XI*, 1973,
transl. A. Sheridan as *The Four Fundamental Concepts of Psycho-
Analysis*, ed. J.-A. Miller, London: Hogarth.

Lacan, J. (1986) L'Ethique de la psychanalyse', in *Le Séminaire de
Jacques Lacan, Livre VII*, Paris: Editions du Seuil.

Langer, S. (1953) *Feeling and Form: A theory of art developed from
philosophy in a new key*, London: Routledge & Kegan Paul.

Lauter, P. (ed.) (1964) *Theories of Comedy*, Garden City, NY: Doubleday/Anchor.

Le Roy Ladurie, E. (1981) *Carnival in Romans*, transl. M. Feeney, Harmondsworth: Penguin.

Leach, E. (1970) *Lévi-Strauss*, London: Fontana/Collins.

Lee, J. S. (1990) *Jaques Lacan*, Boston, MA: Twayne.

Lemaire, A. (1977) *Jaques Lacan*, transl. D. Macey, London: Routledge.

Lerner, L. (ed.) (1967) *Shakespeare's Comedies: An anthology of modern criticism*, Harmondsworth: Penguin.

Lévi-Strauss, C. (1963) *Le Totémisme aujourd'hui*, 1962, transl. R. Needham as *Totemism*, London: Beacon Press.

Lévi-Strauss, C. (1972) *L'Anthropologie structurale*, 1958, transl. Claire Jacobson as *Structural Anthropology* (2 vols), New York: Basic Books; Harmondsworth, Penguin.

Lundberg, C. C. (1969) 'Person-focussed joking: Pattern and function', *Human Organisation*, **28**, 22–8.

McFadden, G. (1982) *Discovering the Comic*, Princeton, NJ: Princeton University Press.

McGhee, P. (1979) *Humor: Its origins and development*, San Francisco, CA: W.H. Freeman.

McGhee, P. and Chapman, A. (1980) *Children's Humour*, Chichester: Wiley.

Mast, G. (1979) *The Comic Mind: Comedy and the movies* (2nd edn), London: University of Chicago Press.

Mehlman, J. (1975) 'How to read Freud on jokes: The critic as Schadchen', *New Literary History*, **16**, 12, 439–61.

Meredith, G. (1885) 'An essay on comedy' (delivered 1877), in *Collected Works*, London: Chapman & Hall.

Moi, T. (1985) *Sexual/Textual Politics: Feminist literary theory*, London: Routledge.

Mulhern, F. (1978) *The Moment of Scrutiny*, London: New Left Books.

Nash, W. (1985) *The Language of Humour*, London: Longman.

Neale, S. (1981) 'Psychoanalysis and comedy', *Screen*, **22**, 2, 29–43.

Nelson, T. G. A. (1990) *Comedy: The theory of comedy in literature, drama and criticism*, London: Oxford University Press.

Neve, M. (1988) 'Freud's theory of humour, wit and jokes', in J. Durant and J. Miller (eds), *Laughing Matters: A serious look at humour*, London: Longman Scientific and Technical, pp. 35–43.

Omwake, L. (1937) 'A study of humour: Its relation to sex, age and personal characteristics', *Journal of Applied Psychology*, **21**, 688–704.

Palmer, D. J. (1984) *Comedy: Developments in criticism*, London: Methuen.

Palmer, J. (1987) *The Logic of the Absurd*, London: British Film Institute.

Pope-Hennessy, U. (1945) *Charles Dickens*, London: Chatto & Windus.

Radcliffe-Brown, A. R. (1940) 'On joking relationships', *Africa*, **13**, 195–210.

Radway, J. (1984) *Reading the Romance: Women, patriarchy and popular literature*, Chapel Hill, NC/London: University of North Carolina Press.

Reader, J. (1990) *Man on Earth*, Harmondsworth: Penguin.

Rice, P. and Waugh, P. (1989) *Modern Literary Theory: A reader*, London: Edward Arnold.

Rigby, P. (1968) 'Joking relationships, kin categories and clanship among the Gogo', *Africa*, **38**, 135–55.

Ryan, K. (1989) *Shakespeare*, Hemel Hempstead: Harvester Wheatsheaf.

Sacks, O. (1985) *The Man Who Mistook His Wife for a Hat*, London: Pan/Picador.

Saussure, F. de (1974) *Cours de linguistique générale*, 1913, transl. W. Baskin as *Course in General Linguistics*, London: Collins/Fontana.

Sinfield, A. (1989) *Literature, Politics and Culture in Postwar Britain*, Oxford: Blackwell.

Spender, D. (1980) *Man Made Language*, London: Routledge & Kegan Paul.

Stallybrass, P. and White, A. (1987) *The Politics and Poetics of Transgression*, London: Methuen.

Sterne, L. (1970) *The Life and Opinions of Tristram Shandy, Gentleman* [1759–66], Harmondsworth: Penguin.

Styan, J. L. (1968) *The Dark Comedy* (2nd edn), Cambridge: Cambridge University Press.

Torrance, R. (1978) *The Comic Hero*, Cambridge, MA: Harvard University Press.

Wade, W. C. (1987) *The Fiery Cross*, New York: Simon & Schuster.

Weber, S. (1977) 'The divaricator: Remarks on Freud's *Witz*', *Glyph*, **1**, 1–27.

Weimann, R. (1987), ed. Robert Schwartz, *Shakespeare and the Popular Tradition in Theatre: Studies in the social dimension of dramatic form and function*, London: Johns Hopkins University Press.

Wellesford, E. (1961) *The Fool*, Garden City, NY: Doubleday/Anchor.

Westcott, J. (1962) 'The sculpture and myths of Eshu-Elegba the Yoruba trickster', *Africa*, **32**, 336–54.

Williams, R. (1976) *Keywords: A vocabulary of culture and society*, London: Fontana.

Winterstein, A. (1934) 'Contributions to the problem of humour', *Psychoanalytic Quarterly*, **3**, 303–15.

Womack, P. (1987) *Ben Jonson*, Oxford: Blackwell.

Zippen, D. (1966) 'Sex differences and the sense of humour', *Psychoanalytic Review*, **53**, 209–19.

Index